Douglas

MOTOR CYCLES

1948 - 1951

Maintenance Manual

Incorporating the Plus Series
and Competition Models

DOUGLAS (SALES & SERVICE) LTD., KINGSWOOD, BRISTOL

Telephone 73013/8   Telegrams: Douglas, Kingswood, Bristol

INTRODUCTION

Welcome to the world of digital publishing ~ the book you now hold in your hand, while unchanged from the original edition, was printed using the latest state of the art digital technology. The advent of print-on-demand has forever changed the publishing process, never has information been so accessible and it is our hope that this book serves your informational needs for years to come. If this is your first exposure to digital publishing, we hope that you are pleased with the results. Many more titles of interest to the classic automobile and motorcycle enthusiast, collector and restorer are available via our website at www.VelocePress.com. We hope that you find this title as interesting as we do.

NOTE FROM THE PUBLISHER

The information presented is true and complete to the best of our knowledge. All recommendations are made without any guarantees on the part of the author or the publisher, who also disclaim all liability incurred with the use of this information.

TRADEMARKS

We recognize that some words, model names and designations, for example, mentioned herein are the property of the trademark holder. We use them for identification purposes only. This is not an official publication.

INFORMATION ON THE USE OF THIS PUBLICATION

This manual is an invaluable resource for the classic motorcycle enthusiast and a "must have" for owners interested in performing their own maintenance. However, in today's information age we are constantly subject to changes in common practice, new technology, availability of improved materials and increased awareness of chemical toxicity. As such, it is advised that the user consult with an experienced professional prior to undertaking any procedure described herein. While every care has been taken to ensure correctness of information, it is obviously not possible to guarantee complete freedom from errors or omissions or to accept liability arising from such errors or omissions. Therefore, any individual that uses the information contained within, or elects to perform or participate in do-it-yourself repairs or modifications acknowledges that there is a risk factor involved and that the publisher or its associates cannot be held responsible for personal injury or property damage resulting from the use of the information or the outcome of such procedures.

WARNING!

One final word of advice, this publication is intended to be used as a reference guide, and when in doubt the reader should consult with a qualified technician.

PREFACE

This Manual, in conjunction with the Illustrated Spares Catalogue, will enable both the private Owner and the motor cycle Dealer to follow the construction and servicing of 1948 to 1951 Douglas machines. It has been compiled primarily for the current Mark V model but the Plus Series, rigid frame Competition and earlier models are described where they differ constructionally.

For ease of reference within this Manual the various models in the ' Mark ' Series have been termed Standard machines. Where handed parts are mentioned these have been viewed from the saddle. As it is customary to work upon the engine from the front, great care must be exercised in identifying handed parts since the general order will, in fact, be reversed. To assist identification of certain components which are illustrated in the Spares Catalogue their plate reference and numbers have been quoted in this Manual.

The most valuable axiom for the amateur mechanic is ' A little knowledge is dangerous.' The greatest enthusiasm cannot replace experience and it is strongly urged that operations are not undertaken unless there is a reasonable possibility of satisfactory completion. The DOUGLAS Specialised Dealer Scheme, augmented by the Factory's Service Department, is available for the provision of Technical information, replacement parts, and the execution of major overhauls or repairs.

Jan. 1951

INDEX

Section	Page
1. General description and technical data	7 and 8
2. ON THE ROAD	
Controls—adjustment	9
Filling up	9
Riding	12
Running-in	13
Starting	11
3. LUBRICATION	
Clutch Cam and Thrust Bearing	16
Engine	15
External points	16
Fork—rear	16
Fork—front	15
Gearbox	15
Speedometer Gearbox	16
Wheels and other grease points	16
4. RUNNING ADJUSTMENTS	
Brakes	21
Carburettors	25
Chain—and care of	24
Clutch Cable and Clutch	20
Cleaning machine	31
Decarbonising	27
Electrical equipment	26
Grinding-in valves	30
Removing carbon	29
Sparking Plugs—cleaning and types	26
Steering Head	22
Tappets	19
Valve—removal	28
Valve—re-fitting	30
Wheel alignment	25
Wheel hubs	22
Wheel removal—front	22
Wheel removal—rear	23
5. COMPLETE OVERHAUL	
Clutch—removal and dismantling	37
Clutch—re-assembly and re-fitting	48
Crankcase—parting	38
Crankcase—re-assembly	42
Crankshaft—examination	40
Cylinder Heads and Cylinders—removal	36
Cylinder Heads—dismantling	40
Cylinders—examination	41
Cylinders and Pistons—re-fitting	43
Cylinder Heads—assembly and re-fitting	45
Douglas Radiadraulic Front Fork	67
Engine dismantling	35
Engine and Gearbox—removal from frame	33

INDEX—*continued*

Section	Page
5. **Complete Overhaul**—*continued*	

Engine
- Engine—separating from gearbox 35
- Engine—re-assembly 42
- Engine—re-fitting to gearbox 58
- Engine and Gearbox—replacing in frame 60
- Final Drive—dismantling 53
- Final Drive Housing—re-fitting 57
- Final re-assembly of engine and gearbox 60
- Front Fork—removal 67
- Front Fork—dismantling 69
- Front Fork—re-assembly 69
- Front Fork—fitting to frame 70

Gearbox
- Gearchange mechanism 58
- Selector mechanism 58
- Dismantling 49
- Shafts and Gears—removal 51
- Sleeve Gear Pinion and Layshaft—re-fitting 55
- Re-assembly 55

- Ignition timing 46
- Kickstart mechanism—re-assembly 56
- Kickstart bevel gear—replacing 57
- Magdyno—removal 36
- Miscellaneous 41
- Oil Pump—removal 40
- Oil Pump—re-fitting 46
- Pistons—removing 36
- Pistons—examination 41
- Pistons and Cylinders—re-fitting 43
- Rear Suspension 62
- Rear Fork and Torsion Bars—removal 63
- Rear Fork and Torsion Bars—re-assembly 65
- Starting after overhaul 62
- Suggestions—preparatory to overhaul 32
- Timing Cover and Gears—removal 37
- Timing Gears—re-assembly 45
- Timing Cover—re-fitting 47
- Wheel Spindles and bearing—dismantling and re-assembly .. 70

6. **FAULT FINDING**

Causes and Remedies
- Carburettor—rich mixture 75
- Excessive oil consumption 76
- H.T. Leads 76
- Ignition System 75
- Noises 77
- Petrol System 75
- Sparking Plugs 75

Charts
- Engine stops of own accord 72
- Engine will not start 73
- Engine runs incorrectly 74

LIST OF ILLUSTRATIONS & TABLES

Fig.		Page
1	Table Identifying Models	7
2	Plan View of Controls	11
3	Lubrication Schedule	17
4	Lubrication Diagram	18
5	Valve Tappet Adjustment	19
6	Clutch Cable Adjustment	21
7	Wheel Alignment	25
8	Removal of Engine Valve	29
9	Removal of Power Unit from Frame	35
10	Removal of Crankshaft	39
11	Crankshaft Assembly with Pistons	41
12	Inserting Flywheel side of Crankshaft into Crankcase	42
13	Crankcase ready for assembly	43
14	Valve Timing Diagram. Standard and Plus Series	44
15	Oil Pump	46
16	Clutch Assembly—Sectioned View, showing Extractor and Holding Plate	48
17	Kickstart Mechanism—Sectional View	51
18	Final Drive—Exploded View	52 and 53
19	Gearbox—Diagrammatic View	54
20	Gearchange Mechanism	59
21	Rear Suspension—Exploded View	64
22	Rear Suspension lever position	66
23	Front Fork—Exploded and Sectional View	68
24, 25 and 26	Fault Finding Graphs	72, 73 and 74

GENERAL DESCRIPTION OF MACHINES

THE DOUGLAS Machines dealt with in this Manual have a 348 c.c. horizontally opposed twin cylinder overhead-valve engine, set transversely in a duplex cradle type frame, and forming a unit with the 'in-line' gearbox. With the exception of the Competition model, they have torsion bar rear suspension of the swinging fork type and bottom link action front forks. The suspension is of unique design and is covered by DOUGLAS patents.

Model	Date of Manufacture	Engine Number & Prefix
Mark III	1948/9 Seasons	T35/S/4,000 onwards/3
Mark III 'Sports'	1948/9 Seasons	T35/S/4,000 onwards/S
Mark IV 'De Luxe'	1950 Season	7,000 onwards/4
Mark IV 'Sports'	1950 Season	7,000 onwards/S4
Mark V	1951 Season	9,000 onwards/5
Competition	1950 Season	Up to 8,978/C
90 Plus	1950 Season	Up to 9,000/90
Competition	1951 Season	8,979 onwards/C
80 Plus	1951 Season	Over 9,000/80
90 Plus	1951 Season	Over 9,000/90

Fig. 1. *Table identifying models*

The engine number is stamped on the top left hand side of the crankcase and the frame number is stamped on the left side of the headlug.

TECHNICAL DATA

Cylinder Bore ... ... 2.394" (60.8 mm.)
Piston Stroke ... ... 2.362" (60.0 mm.)
Total Capacity ... ... 21.24 cubic " (348 c.c.)

	Standard	Plus Series	Competition
Compression Ratio	7.25 : 1	8.25 : 1 (Standard) 9.50 : 1 (Special) 10.50 : 1 (Special)	6.50 : 1
Max. Safe R.P.M.	5,500	7,500	5,000
Petrol Tank Capacity (Main)	3 gallons (13.638 litres)	3 gallons (13.638 litres) 4 gallons (Special) (18.18 litres) 5 gallons (Alloy) (22.73 litres)	2½ gallons (11.36 litres)
Petrol Tank Capacity (Reserve)	3 pints (1.7 litres)	3 pints (1.7 litres)	2 pints (1.13 litres)
Engine Sump Capacity	4 pints (2.27 litres)	4 pints (2.27 litres)	4 pints (2.27 litres)
Gearbox Capacity	1¾ pints (1.0 litre)	1¾ pints (1.0 litre)	1¾ pints (1.0 litre)
O/A Length	84" (213.36 cm.)	84½" (214.63 cm.)	83½" (212.09 cm.)
O/A Height	39¼" (99.7 cm.)	40½" (102.87 cm.)	40" (101.6 cm.)
O/A Width	27½" (69.85 cm.) Mark III and IV 29" (73.66 cm.)	27½" (69.85 cm.)	27½" (69.85 cm.)
Wheel Base	54½" (138.43 cm.)	54½" (138.43 cm.)	54" (137.16 cm.)
Ground Clearance (Loaded)	5¼" (13.335 cm.)	4½" (11.43 cm.)	8" (20.3 cm.)
(Unloaded)	6¼" (15.875 cm.)	5" (12.70 cm.)	8" (20.3 cm.)
Weight (dry with accessories)	365 lbs. (158.757 kg.)	393 lbs. (178.261 kg.)	300 lbs. (136.077 kg.)

Gear Ratios	Standard	80 Plus	90 Plus	Competition
1st. (Low)	15.3 : 1	17.2 : 1	11.48 : 1 Special 9.8 : 1	21.7 : 1
2nd.	10.1 : 1	10.6 : 1	7.78 : 1 Special 7.17 : 1	14.3 : 1
3rd.	7.38 : 1	7.78 : 1	6.68 : 1 Special 6.17 : 1	8.35 : 1 Special 10.5 : 1
4th. (High)	5.86 : 1	6.17 : 1	5.7 : 1	6.6 : 1

The basic reduction in the gearbox (all models) is 1.86 : 1. The top gear of the Standard models may be reduced to 6.19 : 1 by the fitment of an 18T gearbox sprocket.
On the Plus Series Models, the range of gearbox sprockets between 16T and 18T, and rear wheel sprockets between 49T and 57T, provides a top gear variation from 5.06 : 1 to 6.62 : 1.

ON THE ROAD

Filling Up

A quick release filler cap is fitted to the Petrol Tank. To remove, rotate the cap anti-clockwise one quarter of a turn and lift off. To fill the engine sump unscrew the winged cap in the oil filler boss which is situated on the front left hand side of the crankcase. Fill the sump with oil until the level reaches the upper mark of the dipstick. The lower mark on the disptick is a danger mark and in no circumstances should the oil level be allowed to fall below this. The quantity of oil necessary to bring the level in the sump from the danger to the full mark is approximately $1\frac{3}{4}$ pints (1 litre). To fill the gearbox remove the winged cap, incorporating the dipstick, situated on top of the gearbox, and follow the same procedure as for the engine sump. Never allow the oil level to fall below the lower or reach above the higher, mark on the dipstick.

To obtain the most satisfactory service from the machine it is essential that only lubricants of the highest quality be used as recommended on the lubrication schedule, page 17. The use of an upper cylinder lubricant is advisable during the first 1,000 miles (1,600 km.) of the machine's life and may be used regularly thereafter.

Check all the cycle parts and other items requiring lubrication as specified on the schedule on page 17.

Controls

It is advisable before starting the machine to spend some time sitting in the saddle to familiarise oneself with the disposition and operation of the various controls, and the ' feel ' of the machine.

The throttle control is the twist grip on the right handlebar and operates the throttles of both carburettors simultaneously through cable controls and a junction box. To open the throttle the twist grip is turned towards the rider.

There is not a remotely controlled air lever, but a plunger type control is fitted to each carburettor for starting from cold; to operate, press down and turn to the right, thus enriching the mixture. Also on the right handlebar are the horn button and the front brake lever which operates the brake by cable control.

On the left handlebar are the clutch lever, the head-lamp dipper switch, engine (ignition) cut-out button and the manually operated advance and retard ignition control lever.

The footbrake pedal is placed just forward of the left footrest, and the gearchange pedal in the corresponding position on the right hand side of the machine. The kickstarter is placed a little to the rear and above the gearchange pedal and can be operated whilst straddling the machine.

Footbrake, footrests, gearchange, handlebar, control levers, tank, knee grips and saddle are adjustable and should be positioned to suit the requirements of the individual rider so that he may operate each control comfortably and quickly.

These should be adjusted in the following way:—

FOOTBRAKE

The position of the brake pedal, which is controlled by the stop, can be varied by slackening the locknut, (27/52) screwing the adjuster, and relocking with the nut. This will not effect the cable length.

FOOTRESTS

Slacken the $\frac{7}{16}$" B.S.F. nut on the left footrest sufficiently to allow both footrests to turn on the serrations. Adjust as required and tighten the nut.

GEARCHANGE PEDAL

Remove the neutral indicator (17/35), slacken the pinchbolt (17/32), and withdraw the pedal. Refit in desired position and press well back while tightening the pinchbolt. Replace the indicator so that it registers with the button on the footchange cover when the machine is in neutral gear.

HANDLEBAR CONTROL LEVERS

Loosen the pinchscrews, set where required, and tighten screws.

HANDLEBAR

Slacken the 2—$\frac{7}{16}$" B.S.F. nuts (25/6) which secure the links to the lugs, adjust to required height and tighten the nuts. To adjust for wrist angle, slacken the 2—$\frac{1}{4}$" B.S.F. nuts (25/10) turn the handlebar in the eyes of the links and tighten the nuts. The handlebar on the Plus Series can be inverted to provide a downswept position.

PETROL TANK

To elevate or lower the front of the tank, (and with it the knee grips) remove the $\frac{1}{4}$" B.S.F. bolt (30/11) securing tank to headlug, and adjust by using one of the three holes provided in the tank.

KNEE GRIPS

Remove the rubber pads, which are sprung on to plates (30/5), and adjust the plates in any one of the three positions available.

SADDLE

The nose of the saddle can be adjusted to any one of the three positions provided by the holes in the frame bracket. On the Mark IV model the adjustment of the rear of the saddle is obtained by movement of the spring bracket which has three stations. On the Mark V and Plus Series models, the adjustment of the rear of the saddle is by means of distance pieces which can be set either above or below the spring bracket.

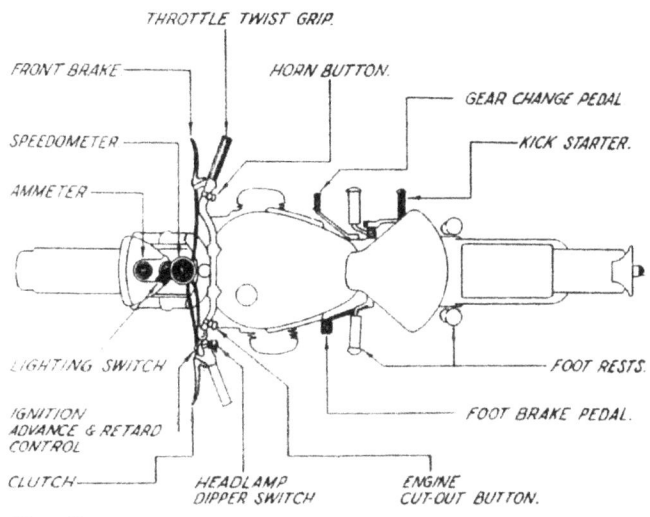

Fig. 2. **PLAN VIEW OF CONTROLS.**

Starting

First ensure that the gear lever is in the neutral position. The petrol taps (one tap only on the Mark III model) which are situated under the tank, each side, should be opened. Pull the round knobs to switch on the main supply and the hexagonal knobs for the reserve supply: note that the reserve taps will not function unless the main supply is left open. Next, slightly flood each carburettor by depressing the tickler on top of the float chamber until the petrol just starts to flow from the vent in the side of the float chamber top. It is important that the carburettors are not over-flooded as this will result in an over rich mixture and starting will be difficult. In normal conditions it will not be found necessary to choke the carburettors with the plungers; if, however, the temperature is very low, it may be advantageous to do this by pressing down each plunger to the extent of its travel and giving a turn to the right, thereby locking the plunger in position. Set the ignition control lever to mid. position and the throttle about one eighth open. Smartly depress the kickstart pedal, do not kick timidly or stop before the pedal has reached the end of its travel: the engine should start after the second or third kick. After a little experience it will be found possible to set the controls to obtain a start 'first kick' result, except in the the very coldest conditions.

If it has been necessary to use the plungers on the carburettors, these must be returned to their original (open) position directly the engine has warmed a little. Never ride any distance with the carburettors choked by the plungers as this will result in excessive petrol consumption and unsatisfactory running.

Never over-rev an engine, especially when starting from cold; always warm up gradually and thus give the oil a chance to circulate freely.

To stop the engine close the throttle and depress the engine ignition cut-out button on the left handlebar. Turn off the petrol.

Riding

To set the machine in motion, engage bottom (first) gear. To do this pull the clutch lever (on the left handlebar) towards you to its fullest extent and with the toe of the right foot, lift the gear change pedal firmly upwards to the full extent of its travel. Now let in the clutch very gently by gradually releasing the lever and, at the same time, increase the engine speed by gradually opening the throttle. This will take the machine smoothly into motion. For the best results it is necessary for all these movements to be carried out firmly and gradually.

To change into a higher gear, accelerate until the correct speed is reached (see table on p. 13) then partially close the throttle and simultaneously withdraw the clutch. This will decrease the engine speed, which is necessary when changing to a higher gear. At the same time depress the gearchange pedal to the extent of its travel and retain it in that position while letting in the clutch. The machine will then be in second gear. Repeat this procedure for changing into third and top gears, and after every gear change allow the pedal, which is spring-loaded, to return to its free (central) position.

To change into a lower gear, withdraw the clutch, accelerate the engine, lift the gearchange pedal to the extent of its travel, and let in the clutch.

As a guide to the beginner, the following speeds are suggested as being suitable for gear changing:—

	Standard Models	Plus Series
First to Second gear	10 m.p.h. (16 km.p.h.)	20 m.p.h. (32 km.p.h.)
Second to Third gear	15 m.p.h. (24 km.p.h.)	25 m.p.h. (40 km.p.h.)
Third to Fourth gear	25 m.p.h. (40 km.p.h.)	30 m.p.h. (48 km.p.h.)

These speeds are approximate and after a time experience will dictate the speeds at which gearchanges can best be made.

To develop a neat and silent gearchange technique may take some time and trouble but this will be amply repaid by greater comfort and longer life for the machine.

Use the throttle to govern the speed of the machine; to lift the clutch and apply the brakes to slow the machine is wasteful when the same braking effect could be obtained by closing the throttle, allowing the engine to retard the machine's speed. On greasy roads the use of the engine as a brake is to be recommended, especially for effecting a smooth change to a lower gear.

To stop the engine after the machine has been brought to a standstill, engage neutral,—a neutral indicator is provided on all models except the Mark III—close the throttle and depress the engine ignition cut-out button on the left handlebar. Turn off the petrol.

Running in

To ensure the best service and length of life from your machine, care should be taken with the running-in. The engine should never be allowed to over-rev or labour and for the first 500 miles (800 km.) it is recommended that the throttle should not be opened more than approximately half way.

The following is given as a guide for all standard models but the Plus Series machines may be given a little greater licence:—

MAXIMUM RUNNING IN SPEEDS

	Up to 200 miles (320 km.)	200 to 400 miles (320 to 640 km.)	400 to 500 miles (640 to 800 km.)
Top gear	35 m.p.h. (55 km.p.h.)	45 m.p.h. (70 km.p.h.)	50 m.p.h. (80 km.p.h.)
3rd. gear	28 m.p.h. (44 km.p.h.)	36 m.p.h. (57 km.p.h.)	40 m.p.h. (64 km.p.h.)
2nd. gear	20 m.p.h. (32 km.p.h.)	26 m.p.h. (42 km.p.h.)	30 m.p.h. (48 km.p.h.)
1st. (Low)	14 m.p.h. (22 km.p.h.)	18 m.p.h. (29 km.p.h.)	20 m.p.h. (32 km.p.h.)

After 500 miles (800 km.) have been covered, short bursts of speed are desirable to hasten the final bedding-down of the pistons. Gradually increase the duration of the speed bursts until the machine will stand large throttle openings for indefinite periods. Running, say, 1,000 miles (1,600 km.) at 30 m.p.h. (48 km.) will not bed down the pistons to enable them to stand continuous high speed running. Piston temperatures are the important factor and this depends not only on speed and throttle opening but also on how long that particular throttle opening has been reasonably sustained.

If the engine shows the slightest sign of slowing, 'pinking,' overheating or seizing, immediately lift the clutch and close the throttle. Serious damage may result to the pistons if the inertia of the machine forces them up and down the cylinders when they are over-expanded, through heat.

We recommend that, after the first 500 miles (800 km.) the machine be returned to the dealer who will carry out a check in accordance with the Douglas Free Service Scheme.

LUBRICATION

Engine Lubrication System

The vane type oil pump driven by a vertical shaft through worm gearing from the right hand camshaft, is situated in the sump and is completely submerged. The pump draws oil through a removable gauze filter and forces it under pressure, through internal passages, to the phosphor bronze (timing side) crankshaft main bearing and thence through drilled oil-holes in the crankshaft to the big end roller bearings. The remainder of the moving parts, including the gudgeon pins, are lubricated by splash and oil mist, the surplus oil draining back to the sump. The normal oil pressure is approximately 6—9 lbs. per square inch (.42—.63 kgm./sq. cm.). The sump should be drained and refilled after the first 500 miles (800 km.) and thereafter every 2,000 miles (3,200 km.). The sump and oil ways may be cleaned by use of one of the various flushing oils; circulate the flushing oil freely by starting the engine, but do not run the engine for more than approximately one minute. Drain and refill with fresh lubricating oil as recommended. Providing these simple instructions are carried out the rider should never experience trouble from the lubrication system.

Gearbox

After the gearbox has been filled with the recommended oil to the required level, it is only necessary to keep up the level, and drain and refill at the specified intervals. To drain, unscrew the plug situated in the right hand side of the gearbox, taking care not to lose the fibre washer on the plug. The recommended grades of lubricant are shown in the schedule.

Front Fork

Check the oil level in the fork legs every 3,000 miles (4,800 km.) by removing the level plugs at the rear of the link bearing housings. The viscosity of the oil used will vary the damping effect of the fork. The grades stated in the Lubrication Schedule are the lowest viscosity permitted and are generally most suitable. To top-up, unscrew the countersunk head screw set into the centre of the bolt on top of each fork leg and pour in, slowly, sufficient oil to bring the level coincident with the level plug. Replace level plugs and filler screws. To drain the fork, remove the aluminium bottom end caps from the fork legs.

After each 1,000 miles (1,600 km.) apply the grease gun to:—

(a) The grease nipples on the steering head lug and column.
(b) ,,   ,,   ,,   ,,   ,, brake torque link.
(c) ,,   ,,   ,,   ,,   ,, mudguard stay link (Mark IV onwards).

Rear Swinging Fork

(EXCLUDING COMPETITION MODELS)

There are four grease nipples each side of the rear suspension system. Two of these are in full sight and readily accessible, being located in the end cap for the pivot pin and in the lever attached to the rear end of the torsion bar. The remaining two are in the pivot bolts for the link connecting the lever to the fork. The top one of these is cranked and obscured by the channel section of the fork. The grease gun should be applied to the nipples on both sides of the machine every 1,000 miles (1,600 km.).

Wheel and other grease points

One stroke of the grease gun should be applied to each hub and the front and rear brake cam spindles every 2—3,000 miles (3,200—4,800 km.). Care should be taken not to use too much as excessive grease will work its way into the brakes, impairing their efficiency. The grease gun should also be applied to the following points, in accordance with the Lubrication Schedule:—

Clutch Cam and Thrust Bearing. Remove the inspection cover (or air funnel on Plus Series models) situated on the left hand side of the clutch housing. An extension nipple can be fitted to the Mark III and Mark III Sports models.

Speedometer gearbox situated on the right hand side of the rear wheel.

External Points

Use engine oil, in an oil can, every 2,000 miles (3,200 km.) on the following:—Handlebar control levers, control cables, front brake anchorage plate (through the small grub-screw hole in the upper side of the central boss), saddle pivot bolt, rear brake pedal, pillion footrests, front mudguard stays at wheel spindle (Mark IV models onwards but not Plus Series) and folding kickstart pedal (if fitted).

Attention Required	Standard Models		Plus Series Models
	Summer	Winter	Summer and Winter
ENGINE Inspect level in sump every 200 miles (320 km.). Drain and refill at first 500 miles (800 km.) and thereafter 2,000 miles (3,200 km.)	Mobiloil D Castrol XXI Essolube 50 Triple Shell	Mobiloil A Castrol XL Essolube 40 Double Shell	Mobiloil D Castrol Grand Prix Essolube Racer Golden Shell
GEARBOX Inspect level every 1,000 miles (1,600 km.) Drain and refill every 10,000 miles (16,000 km.)	Mobiloil D Castrol ST Essolube gear oil, Medium Golden Shell		Mobiloil BB Castrol XL Essolube 40 Double Shell
FRONT FORK Check oil level in each fork leg every 3,000 miles (4,800 km.)	**ALL MODELS** Mobiloil Arctic. Castrolite. Essolube 20. Single Shell Retinax RB. Heavier oil may be used to increase damping		
Grease Gun. Mobilgrease No. 2. Castrolease CL. Esso Grease. Shell Retinax RB.			
Every 1,000 miles (1,600 km.). Steering Columnn (2). Front Brake and Mudguard Links (4). Rear Suspension (8).			
Every 2,000 miles (3,200 km.). Wheel Hubs (2). Brake Cam Spindles (2). Speedometer Gearbox (1). Clutch Cam and Thrust Bearing (1).			
Oil Can (Engine Oil). Every 2,000 miles (3,200 km.). Control Levers and Cables, Front Brake Anchorage Plate, Mudguard Anchorage Plate (Plus Series), Saddle Pivot, Rear Brake Pedal, Pillion Footrests, Mudguard Stays, Folding Kickstart Pedal.			

Fig. 3. *Lubrication Schedule*

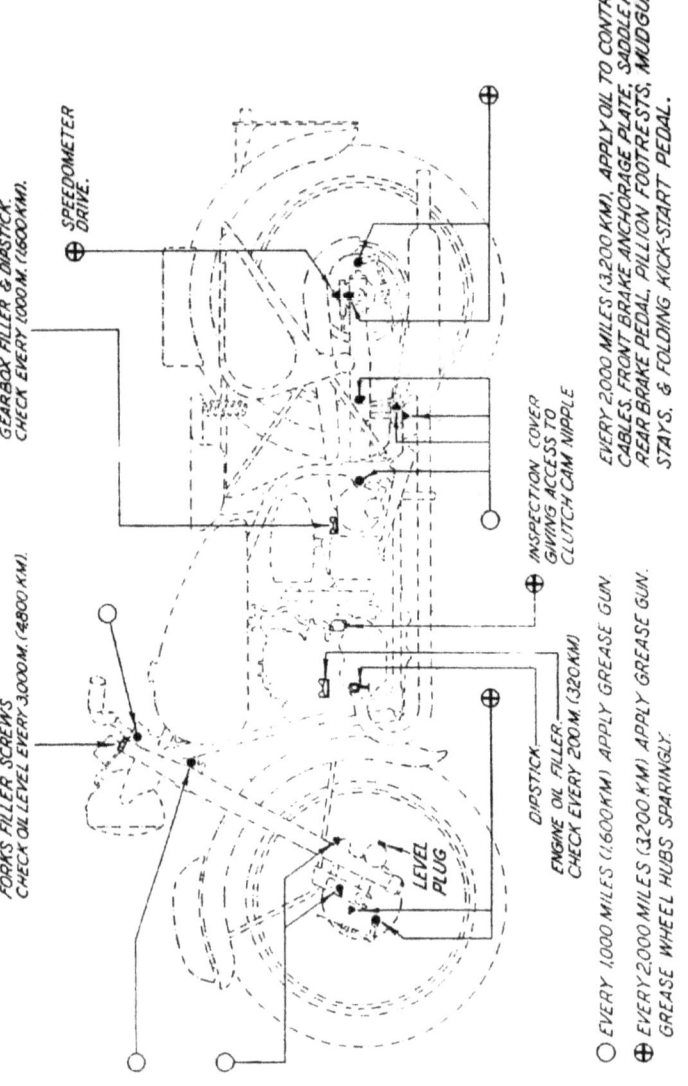

Fig. 4. LUBRICATION DIAGRAM.

RUNNING ADJUSTMENTS AND GENERAL MAINTENANCE

After the first 500 miles (800 km.) it is essential that all nuts, especially those on the cylinder heads, are checked and tightened if necessary.

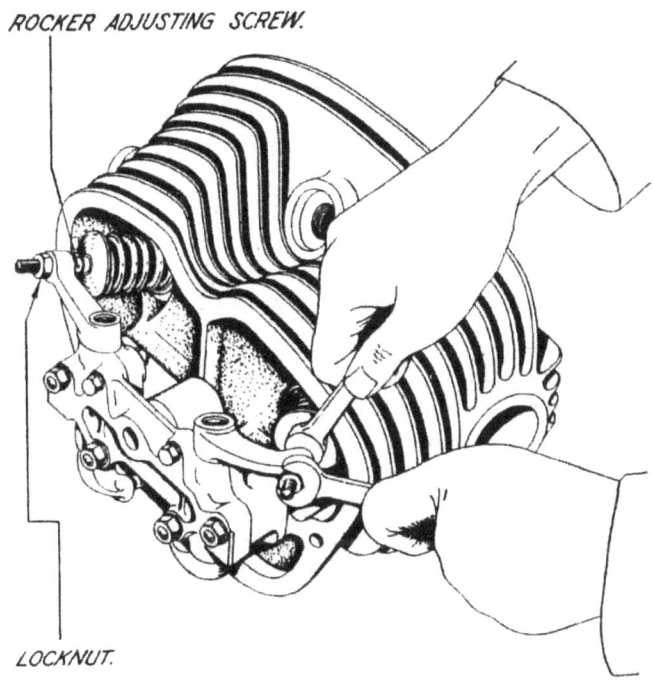

Fig. 5.   VALVE TAPPET ADJUSTMENT.

Tappet Adjustment

To adjust valve clearances, remove the polished aluminium rocker covers (8/26) by undoing the central screws with the tool provided (34/12). With the sparking plugs removed and the machine on the stand, engage top gear and revolve the engine by turning the rear wheel until the engine is at approximately Top Dead Centre (T.D.C.) with both valves of the cylinder under observation closed (the valves of the other cylinder will be ' rocking '). The clearance between the rocker adjusting screw (8/20) and the valve tip should be

.005" (.1250 mm.) on all Standard and Competition models but on the Plus Series machines it should be .025" (.6025 mm.). The engine should be cold when checking tappets and a feeler gauge used. If the clearance requires adjusting, slacken the locknut (8/21) on the rocker adjusting screw and set with a spanner; be sure to lock the nut securely without overstressing. Re-check the clearance, as it is possible that the tightening of the locknut may alter the clearances slightly. Similarly, check and adjust, if necessary, the clearance of the valves in the other cylinder, after making sure that the engine has been rotated one complete revolution to ensure that the valves to be adjusted are closed. Valve adjustment should not be necessary more frequently than at intervals of 2,000 miles (3,200 km.). It is essential that the joint washer (8/27) be renewed if any sign of tearing is detected.

Clutch Cable Adjustment and Clutch

This is effected by the adjuster on the clutch cable which is situated on the left hand side of the crankcase bell housing. The locknut, on the adjuster, should be slackened prior to adjustment and locked after. The machine leaves the Works with the adjuster screwed out to its maximum as any wear that takes place is compensated by screwing the adjuster *in* or *downwards*.

If there is any tendency of the clutch to slip, the adjuster should be screwed inwards until there is approximately $\frac{8}{16}"$ to $\frac{1}{4}"$ (5—6.5 mm.) free movement of the clutch handlebar lever.

Should there be any excessive amount of backlash (free movement) of the clutch handlebar lever or if the clutch does not completely disengage, the adjuster should be screwed outwards.

A remote coarse adjustment is also provided by the swinging movement of the adjustable arm (14/8) on the clutch cam. If necessary this can be reset by removing the inspection cover (or air funnel on the Plus Series machines) and slackening the $\frac{8}{16}"$ B.S.F. bolt and nut, so that the cable adjuster is screwed out fully when the wire has the correct clearance.

The clutch springs are non-adjustable as the rate of wear on the friction linings is very slight. Any wear that does occur is automatically compensated by the clutch springs, and provided the cable is maintained in correct adjustment to keep the necessary clearance for the thrust race bearing, no further adjustment is necessary until relining. (See ' Overhaul ').

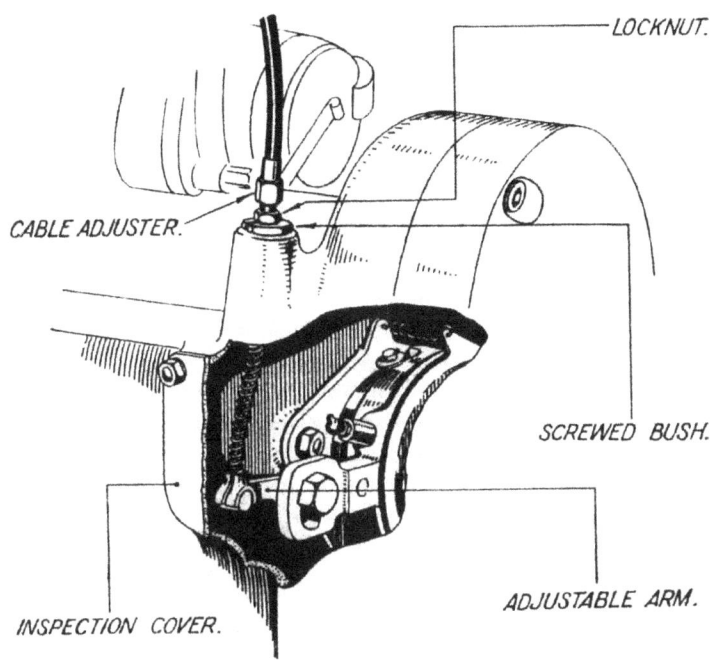

Fig. 6.   *CLUTCH CABLE ADJUSTMENT.*

Brakes

Before attempting to adjust the brakes ensure that the wheels are off the ground.

When adjusting the brakes, avoid an undue amount of slack in the rear brake pedal and the front brake handlebar lever, but make sure the brakes are not binding and that the wheels are perfectly free.

REAR BRAKE ADJUSTMENT

An adjuster and locknut, at the rear end of the cable, controls the rear brake adjustment. On all models, except the Mark III and the Mark III Sports, a pedal stop (27/51) is provided but brake cable adjustment does not vary the positioning of the pedal, nor does varying the pedal position alter the cable adjustment.

FRONT BRAKE ADJUSTMENT

The front brake is adjusted in the same way, by adjuster and locknut, at the wheel end of the cable.

Wheel Hubs

The wheel hubs are fitted with non-adjustable ball bearings, and should require no adjustment after the machine has left the Works.

Adjustment of Steering Head

The steering head should not require adjustment for many thousands of miles, but when play does develop the following procedure should be adopted.

Remove the aluminium dome nut, washer and speedometer, on its bracket, then tighten down the adjustable cone (24/5) until all play in the steering head has been taken up. Care should be taken to ensure that the fork can still swing freely without any signs of tightness. Measure, with the aid of a feeler gauge, the clearance between the shims and the top bridge plate (24/8), then take off the bridge plate by removing the 2 securing bolts (24/12) at the top of each fork leg. Now fit to the steering column, shims to the thickness which has been measured with the feeler gauge. Replace the bridge plate, speedometer bracket, washer and dome nut. Shims are available in the following thicknesses, .0148", .028" and .064" (.376 mm., .711 mm. and 1.626 mm.).

Removal of Front Wheel

It is seldom that either wheel need be removed but should this become necessary, first detach the front brake cable from the handle-bar lever and the clip on the left hand fork leg. The mudguard should now be removed from its stays by taking out the four ¼" B.S.F. bolts and nuts with their flat and shakeproof washers. The guard can now be lifted away, bringing it forward. Remove the two 2 B.A. bolts, nuts and shakeproof washers securing the left hand stay to its bracket, and withdraw the stay. Remove the bolt (24/51) at the fork end of the brake torque link. Slacken—but do not remove—the pinchbolt (24/25) in the right hand wheel link, and remove the wheel spindle nut (26/20). Remove the wheel spindle and take out the wheel, leaving the right hand stay and linkage connected to the fork. If necessary, the brake anchorage plate together with the shoes, mudguard stay and link, can now be lifted from the wheel.

Re-assembly is a reversal of the above procedure but care should be exercised to ensure that the large facing washer (26/44) is replaced upon the head end of the wheel spindle and that the correct number of shims (26/21), if any, for the wheel spindle nut are fitted. On the Mark IV and IV Sports and early Mark V models, the facing washers are slotted to register with dogs in the wheel spindle head but current machines have plain heads to the spindles and flat facing washers are used.

The preceding remarks do not apply to the Mark III, Mark III Sports, Competition or Plus Series machines. On the Mark III, Mark III Sports, and Competition models, the method of removing the wheel is as explained above but the mudguard is not attached to the wheel spindle and need not be removed. On the Plus Series, the procedure is the same but the mudguard stays are connected to the brake anchorage plate, and the right hand stay carrier, by eight $\frac{1}{4}''$ B.S.F. setscrews, flat and shakeproof washers.

Removal of Rear Wheel

With the exception of the Competition Model, which has a rod-operated brake, the method of removing the rear wheel is similar on all models. Remove the chainguard which is secured by one $\frac{1}{4}''$ B.S.F. bolt with a plain and shakeproof washer at the front end, and by two (on the Mark V, one only) $\frac{1}{4}''$ B.S.F. nuts and washers fixing it to the brake anchorage plate. The silencers on the Mark IV Sports, Mark V, and Plus Series models should be removed. Disconnect the speedometer cable from the gearbox on the rear wheel and remove the chain connecting link, taking care not to lose the components. To remove the brake cable take the operating lever 27/27) away from the cam spindle by unscrewing the $\frac{3}{8}''$ B.S.F. nut with its shakeproof washer. The lever can be prised off and the cable adjuster unscrewed from the anchorage plate, after the locknut has been slackened but not unscrewed. This nut position will enable correct brake adjustment to be held for re-assembly.

Finally, remove the $\frac{1}{2}''$ B.S.F. bolt and flat washer which fixes the anchorage plate to the rear fork (rear lug on the Competition models) and slacken the wheel nuts. The chain adjuster nuts should not be disturbed and the chain adjusters complete will come away with the wheel.

The brake rod on the Competition model should be disconnected before the wheel is removed.

Re-fitting Rear Wheel

Replacing the rear wheel is a reversal of the above procedure and, since the chain adjuster nuts have not been disturbed, the wheel will be correctly positioned by simply pressing the adjuster caps against the fork ends. Prior to this, the $\frac{1}{2}''$ B.S.F. bolt and flat washer should be entered into the anchorage plate (but not tightened) and the chain connecting link replaced, taking care that the closed end of the spring clip is facing the direction of the chain travel. Tighten the wheel nuts and anchorage plate bolt, re-fit the speedometer cable and chainguard. Replace the cable adjuster and to engage the brake lever on the square spindle, use a $\frac{3}{16}''$ spanner which will fit the spindle, and turn it to register with the lever.

If difficulty is encountered the operation will be eased by slackening the cable adjuster locknut, allowing more free wire length, but the rear brake will then need re-adjusting. At this stage, it is desirable to check the chain adjustment and wheel alignment as described later.

Chain

The chain should be allowed approximately $\frac{3}{4}''$ up and down play when measured mid-way between the front and rear sprockets. If there is any appreciable variation in its tension throughout one complete revolution of the rear wheel, the chain should be renewed. *It is essential that the correct 'play' is allowed at the tightest point of the chain and the machine should be off its stand for this check.*

The wheel spindle nuts, the nut(s) securing the chainguard to the anchor plate, and the $\frac{1}{2}''$ B.S.F. bolt fixing the anchor plate to the fork, must be slackened prior to varying the chain adjusters. It is advisable to pull up the chain adjuster nuts finally, after the wheel nuts have been secured.

The chain is not automatically lubricated as it is not advisable to oil from the outside—this would only encourage collection of abrasive road grit, etc. It is advantageous to remove the chain, say, every 3,000 miles (4,800 km.), wash it in petrol, and soak in graphited oil overnight. After allowing to drain, it should be wiped with a rag prior to re-fitting. Remember that the closed end of the connecting link spring clip MUST be pointing in the direction of the chain travel.

CHAIN SIZES AND LENGTHS

Standard	80 Plus	90 Plus	Competition
$\frac{1}{2}'' \times .305''$ 12.7 × 7.75 mm. 116 links	$\frac{5}{8}'' \times \frac{1}{4}''$ 15.875 × 6.350 mm. 96 links	$\frac{5}{8}'' \times \frac{1}{4}''$ 15.875 × 6.350 mm. 94 links	$\frac{5}{8}'' \times \frac{1}{4}''$ 15.875 × 6.350 mm. 91 links

The above chain lengths are applicable when standard sprocket sizes are used

Wheel Alignment

To check the wheel alignment, the simplest method is to use a cord or a long true straight edge, in the manner illustrated in Fig. 7. If any adjustment is necessary, slacken off the rear wheel spindle nuts, brake anchorage bolt and chainguard retaining nut(s) and align the wheel by use of the chain adjuster, ensuring that the correct chain tension is maintained. The Competition and Plus Series models have varying tyre sizes and allowance must be made for this equally on each side of the front wheel, which has the smaller section tyre.

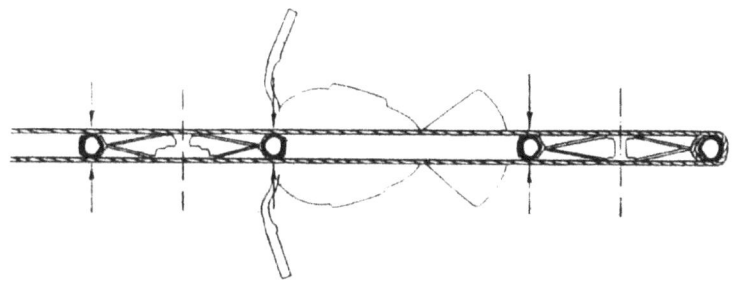

Fig. 7. WHEEL ALIGNMENT.

TYRE SIZE AND INFLATION TABLE

		Standard	Plus Series	Competition
FRONT	Size	3.25"—19" (82 × 483 mm.)	3.00"—21" (76 × 533 mm.)	2.75"—21" (70 × 533 mm.)
	Pressure	22 lbs./sq. " (1.5468 atmhs.)	23 lbs./sq. " (1.6171 atmhs.)	22 lbs./sq. " (1.5468 atmhs.)
REAR	Size	3.25"—19" (82 × 483 mm.)	3.25"—19" (82 × 483 mm.)	4.00"—19" (102 × 483 mm.)
	Pressure	22 lbs./sq. " (1.5468 atmhs.)	22 lbs./sq. " (1.5468 atmhs.)	16 lbs./sq. " (1.1249 atmhs.)

The Inflation pressures refer only for Road Use
For Trials or Speed Events, consult Tyre Manufacturers

Carburettors

Full details of adjustment, tuning, etc., are given in the AMAL leaflet supplied with the machine. It is most important that the throttles open simultaneously and this should be achieved by very careful setting of the control cable adjusters on the carburettors, after each cylinder has been adjusted for 'idling' by the throttle stop (9/20) and pilot air adjusting screw (9/19). There is a further cable adjuster, with locknut, on the front of the junction box under the petrol tank, and this should be used for final adjustment of the throttle control cable.

It is not necessary to vary the main jet sizes if an air cleaner is fitted.

CARBURETTOR SETTINGS

	Standard and Competition	80 Plus 90 Plus
R.H. Carburettor type	274 AJ/4A	276 EB/1B
L.H. Carburettor type	274 AK/4A	276 EQ/1B
Main Jet size	80	130
Throttle Slide	4/5	6/3
Jet Needle	4	6

For information relating to the setting of the T.T. type carburettors (fitted to special order on Plus Series Models) apply to our Technical Department

Electrical Equipment

IGNITION AND LIGHTING

Full details of the Ignition and Lighting equipment are contained in the LUCAS Handbook issued with the machine.

Sparking Plugs

Examine and clean the sparking plugs every 1,000 miles (1,600 km.). Disconnect the H.T. leads from the plugs by pulling off the bakelite waterproof covers, and remove the plugs from the cylinders by using a box spanner on the hexagon of the body and *not* on the gland nut. When dismantling the plug, it is preferable to use two box spanners; the one for the gland nut may be held in a vice.

When withdrawing the body of the electrode it is important to avoid losing the internal gas seal washer. The carbon deposit should be scraped off the inside of the body and cleaned away from the insulator, care being taken not to chip or damage the surface of the ceramic insulator. Rinse the components in clean petrol and dry off. The plug can now be re-assembled, making sure that the gas seal washer is in place.

To adjust the gap, lightly tap the points of the plug towards the central electrode until the correct gap of .015" to .018" (.384 to .461 mm.) is obtained. In no circumstances should the gap be adjusted by bending the central electrode as this will result in damage to the insulator.

It is advisable to renew the sparking plugs every 10,000 miles (16,000 km.) using the type recommended.

RECOMMENDED SPARKING PLUGS

Standard and Competition	Plus Series (Road use)	Plus Series (Speed events)
Lodge H.14	Lodge HH.14 (Replacing HHN)	Lodge R.49 Lodge R.50

Decarbonising

This should be carried out approximately every 5,000 miles (8,000 km.), on the Standard and Competition models. The Plus Series machines, having a higher compression ratio and performance, should receive the same attention at approximately 3,500 miles (5,600 km.).

The following procedure should be adopted:—

Disconnect the exhaust pipes, with silencer(s) from the cylinder heads and frame. The Plus Series machines have screwed gland nuts with C & A washers securing the pipes to the exhaust ports and these should be unscrewed with a 'C' spanner, which is available through the Dealer or direct from the Factory Spares Department.

It is advisable, at this stage, to wipe the carburettors to remove any loose dirt from the exterior. It is also advisable to clean the area around the joints which are to be broken so as to prevent dirt entering the interior.

Disconnect the petrol feed pipes at carburettors, and the carburettors from the induction flanges of the cylinder heads, taking care not to damage the joint washers. Remove air cleaner unit (if fitted), dismantle the filter and clean the element in clean petrol. Do not oil the element.

Unscrew the centre screws and remove the rocker covers, paying careful attention to the joint washers to ensure these are not damaged.

Disconnect H.T. leads from sparking plugs, and sparking plugs from cylinder heads.

Turn the engine until the valves on one cylinder are closed (both valves will be then rocking on the other cylinder). Remove the $\frac{1}{4}''$ B.S.F. nut and washer underneath the push rod tunnel (6/6) and the 4—$\frac{3}{8}''$ B.S.F. cylinder head retaining nuts (8/4) with their split washers. The head should now be free to tap off by hand (if gummed on, wait until the cylinder is removed, when the head can be tapped off the cylinder by inserting a piece of hard wood in the bore).

When the head is off, take out the push rods (6/4), ensuring that they are marked to enable them to be returned to their original stations; a card marked and pierced by the push rod will suffice. Before removing the opposite cylinder head, revolve the engine until the valves are seated and then proceed as with the first head.

Remove the 6—$\frac{5}{16}''$ B.S.F. cylinder base nuts and washers of each cylinder with the cranked double ended spanner supplied in the tool kit. Draw the cylinders off, taking care not to let the pistons fall as they come out. The brass shims between the cylinders and the crankcase should be removed with the cylinders, otherwise the tappets may become detached from their guides, thus losing their location. On the Plus Series, the shim(s) under the cylinders must be returned to their original side. Each cylinder should be marked for assembly on the correct side.

Valve Removal

Unless there is excessive wear in the rockers, the split bearing assemblies (8/22) need not be disturbed to remove the valves. It is necessary to employ a valve spring compression tool (an example is illustrated in Fig. 8) in order to clear the split valve collets (8/17). Care should be exercised in keeping the collets with the respective valves, collars and cups to ensure that they are correctly mated in re-assembly. Although the inlet and exhaust valves are interchangeable on the Standard models, they should not become mixed.

On the Plus Series, steel shim washers replace the cups fitted under the triple valve springs to regulate the fitted length of the springs. It is desirable that the correct fitted length of 1.201" (30.510 mm.) be maintained. The coils of the Plus Series valve springs are closer at one end and these ends should be fitted against the cylinder heads. The inlet valves are semi-tulip and are larger than the exhaust valves.

On the later models of the Plus Series, the valves, collars, collets and valve guides are not interchangeable with those of the earlier models, and if any renewals are made, care must be taken to ensure that the parts are identical with those being replaced.

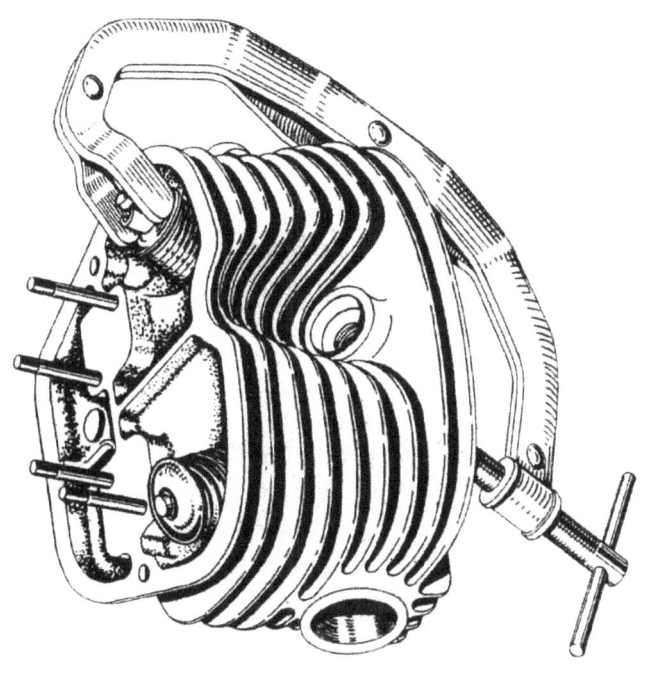

Fig. 8.   REMOVAL OF ENGINE VALVE.

REMOVING CARBON

Carefully scrape the carbon off the piston crowns, polish with metal polish and wash off with clean petrol. Do not use emery cloth.

Clean the carbon out of the cylinder heads and ports, using a round wire-brush and a blunt scraper. Polish the inside of the head with fine emery cloth, taking care not to touch the valve seats. Remove the carbon from the valves, taking care not to scratch or mark the seats. Polish the valve stems with fine emery, soaked in paraffin. Wash valves in petrol.

EXAMINE

Valves (stem or seat wear).
Valve guides (wear).
Fit of the pistons on the gudgeon pins.
Fit of the gudgeon pins in small end bushes.
Rings in grooves (up and down play).
Ring gaps, in cylinders (Max. gap, .012" or .3048 mm.). Rings should be carefully removed from the pistons for this and replaced in the same positions. New rings should have a gap of .006" or .1524 mm.
Pistons (condition of skirts).
Cylinders (wear, scores).
Connecting rod play at big end bearings.

Should any of these show signs of excessive wear or play they should be renewed.

GRINDING-IN VALVES

To grind in a valve, first make sure that the seat is clean, then smear a small quantity of medium grade grinding paste over the valve seat. Put the valve into its correct station in the cylinder head (taking care that the grinding paste does not reach the valve stem) and with the aid of a Suction Cup valve tool, turn the valve with a semi-rotary motion, applying gentle pressure. Lift the valve off its seat at every third or fourth reversal, frequently changing its position. When the face of the valve and the seat in the cylinder head are uniform, repeat, using fine grade grinding paste.

If either the valve faces or the seats in the cylinder heads are badly pitted they should be re-faced—an operation which should be entrusted to the DOUGLAS Dealer.

RE-FITTING VALVES

When all the valves are ground in, wash them and the cylinder heads to ensure that no grinding paste is left. Re-assemble as follows:—

Smear the valve stem with oil and fit to its original position in the cylinder head, put on the spring assembly with the cup or shims (the assembly comprises two springs for every model except the Plus Series which have three) and collar. Compress the spring, with the tool, and re-place the split collets.

FITTING CYLINDERS

The cylinder barrels can now be fitted; see that the brass joint shims at the base are not damaged. Examine the tappets for wear at the feet and for fit in the guides, then carefully put the cylinders on the pistons (after smearing the pistons and cylinder walls with clean engine oil), easing each ring into the bore. It will be helpful if a ring clamp is made up of sheet metal, sufficiently wide to cover two of the three piston rings together. Do not use jointing cement on the brass shims. Each cylinder should now be secured with the six base nuts—the one long nut (2/33) being fitted to the top of the left hand cylinder, near the clutch inspection cover.

FITTING CYLINDER HEADS

The 1948 Mark III and Mark III Sports models were fitted with copper cylinder head gaskets, as are the current Plus Series models. If these are to be re-used they should be annealed. All later Standard models have soft head gaskets and these can be fitted in place of the copper joints on the earlier models. Replace the push rods, ensuring that they locate in the tappets, with the headed ends to the rockers, and that the cams are not lifting the tappets. The cylinder head can now be carefully fitted, taking care not to jam the push rods. It is important, when tightening down the cylinder head nuts with their split washers, first to see that all the nuts are just gripping. Then tighten the four main nuts, working evenly around the head.

The small nut under the push rod tunnel should be left until the four main nuts are tightened. Make sure that the push rods seat in the sockets of the rockers. Check valve tappet clearances and after applying a quantity of oil to the rockers, re-fit rocker covers. Finally, replace cleaned sparking plugs, carburettors, (making sure that the joint washers are in good condition) and the air cleaner (if fitted). If an air leak is suspected at the carburettor joints reference should be made to Section 5 ' Complete Overhaul,' page 61. Re-fit the exhaust pipes, connect up the H.T. leads and petrol pipes.

Cleaning

The appearance and value of the machine will be greatly enhanced if careful and regular attention is paid to cleaning. When enamelled, chromium plated or polished parts are covered with dried mud, never attempt to clean the machine without first soaking the dirt with warm soapy water, then wash off with a hose or sponge and wipe the parts dry with a clean soft duster. After this the frame and chrome parts may be polished with any of the reputable polishes and chrome cleaners available. Failure to soak off carefully any mud will result in the enamel being scratched, and consequent flaking off. If a hose is used, be careful to direct this away from wheel hubs, Magdyno and other delicate parts likely to suffer damage due to the ingress of water. Wheel spokes may be cleaned with a soft brush after soaking. To clean the engine, and any oily surfaces of the machine, wipe with paraffin, wash with water, then dry thoroughly. Occasionally paint the cylinders and heads with a good cylinder heat-resisting black, after removing any mud and oil. Air-drying paint, matching the DOUGLAS colour schemes can be used for touching up and can be obtained from DOUGLAS Dealers or direct from the Factory Spares Department.

COMPLETE OVERHAUL

Suggestions

(1) A useful practice when removing any component from the machine is to temporarily replace all bolts, nuts, washers and screws to prevent loss and to label components to ensure that they are re-fitted in their correct positions.

(2) Before commencing to dismantle the machine (or any part thereof) it is advisable to remove as much mud and dirt as possible. This should be done outside the workshop, thus helping to maintain cleanliness.

(3) When carrying out a major job it will be found more convenient if the machine is placed on a firm platform approximately 15"—18" (38 cm.—46 cm.) high. This will obviate unnecessary stooping.

(4) For ease in handling the engine after removal from the frame, it is suggested that a suitable stand be made in the following way:—

Use two pieces of 2" x 2" (50.8 mm.) angle steel drilled with a $\frac{7}{16}$" (11.11 mm.) hole in the centre of each, and $\frac{1}{2}$" (12.7 mm.) from the edge. Secure the angles to the bench, spaced to allow the crankcase to fit between, and use the front engine mounting bolt to hold the engine.

(5) When dismantling, all small parts removed should be placed in boxes allocated for each particular assembly.

(6) Where tools are necessary in addition to those supplied, the use of ring or box spanners is recommended.

(7) The following special tools are available from the Douglas Dealer or the Factory Spares Department.

    1. Flywheel extractor complete with holding plate for flywheel.

    2. Universal extractor for withdrawing pinions from magneto, camshaft and crankshaft.

    3. 'C' spanner for exhaust gland nuts on Plus Series.

The use of the illustrated Spares Catalogue in conjunction with this Manual will assist in the work.

Removal of Engine—Gearbox Unit from Frame

Drain off engine oil *via* the drain plug (2/26) provided in the left hand side of the sump and re-fit and tighten the drain plug, with its fibre washer.

Remove the petrol tank by adopting the following procedure:— Unfasten the clips securing the saddle top to its frame on the front right hand side and remove the $\frac{5}{18}$" B.S.F. locknut and bolt (31/3) holding the nose of the saddle to the frame. Remove the 2—$\frac{5}{16}$" B.S.F. setscrews and washers retaining the bridge strap (30/18) and detach the petrol pipes at the taps. Slacken the $\frac{1}{4}$" B.S.F. nut ($\frac{5}{16}$" on models prior to Mark IV) securing the nose of the tank, and remove the 2—$\frac{5}{16}$" B.S.F. setscrews securing the underside of the tank to the frame. These setscrews, which are drilled and wired together, each carry a flat washer, voltage control bracket, fibre washer and rubber buffer, in that order.

Remove the bolt holding the nose of the tank (this is held in a rubber sleeve on the models Mark IV onwards) and lift off the tank.

On the Plus Series models fitted with the special four gallon tank, it is also necessary to remove the front fork bridge plate. Remove exhaust pipes and silencer(s).

Disconnect the carburettor controls by unscrewing the ring nuts (9/14) thus obviating any necessity for adjustment on re-assembly. These control wires should be laid over the top frame tube. Remove air cleaner unit if fitted. Disconnect the petrol pipes from float chambers and remove the two retaining nuts at each carburettor flange. When withdrawing carburettors from the cylinder heads, take care not to damage the joint washers. Disconnect accumulator leads at their rubber sleeved couplings and remove accumulator by unscrewing the nuts holding the top strap of the carrier.

On the Mark III model, it is necessary to remove the automatic voltage control unit (12/33) which is situated on the front of the tool box, and to remove the tool box by unscrewing the 4—$\frac{1}{4}$" B.S.F. retaining bolts and nuts. In doing this, care should be taken to retain the two stiffening pieces securing the box, and the two for the voltage control unit, which are inside the tool box.

Remove the two earthing wires from the body of the Magdyno by slackening the grub screw, and the two leads to the dynamo which are retained by a central screw and plate. Remove the screw and withdraw the plate and wires. It will be noted that the plate is curved, the radius following the diameter of the dynamo, in order that the wires may be correctly stationed upon re-fitting. Remove the bakelite contact breaker cover with the lead to the handlebar earthing button attached. The Voltage Control Unit, together with the other wires, may now be laid over the top frame tube and tied.

Remove the shock absorber cover (32/6) by unscrewing the two retaining nuts and washers, and remove the chain, taking care to replace the connecting link on to the chain. Detach the spring from the stand and the accumulator carrier from the gearbox, ensuring that the two spacers are not lost from the bottom setscrews (Mark IV onwards).

Remove the right hand crash bar (if fitted) and the clutch and ignition cables from the handlebar levers. Unclip the cables from the top tube and coil them to prevent damage.

Before attempting to remove the footrest spindle (22/2), which also serves as the rear mounting bolt for the gearbox, place a block of wood of suitable height beneath the gearbox to take the weight of the rear end of the power unit. The left footrest can now be removed by unscrewing the $\frac{7}{16}$" B.S.F. nut and washer. The right footrest can now be withdrawn with the bolt, when two distance pieces (20/11 and 20/12) and the packing shims (20/13) situated between the frame and the gearbox, will fall away. It is essential that the distance pieces and the shims are replaced in the original places as they control the positioning of the gearbox in the frame.

The Plus Series have no tubular distance pieces or shims but, in their place, adjustable separators. The adjustment should not be moved, but upon re-fitting they should be set to provide a snug fit between the frame and the gearbox.

The only attachment now holding the engine and gearbox to the frame is a bolt (20/8) running through the base of the crankcase sump and two brackets on the bottom frame tubes. Before proceeding further, place a support under the crankcase. Remove the $\frac{7}{16}''$ B.S.F. nut and tap out the bolt. It will be found that there are two spacing washers (20/7) between the frame and the engine—these should be replaced on the bolt for safe keeping.

To remove the power unit from the frame it will be necessary to handle as shown in Fig. 9. The unit is taken forward, as far as possible in the frame, and the rear is lifted and brought out to the right.

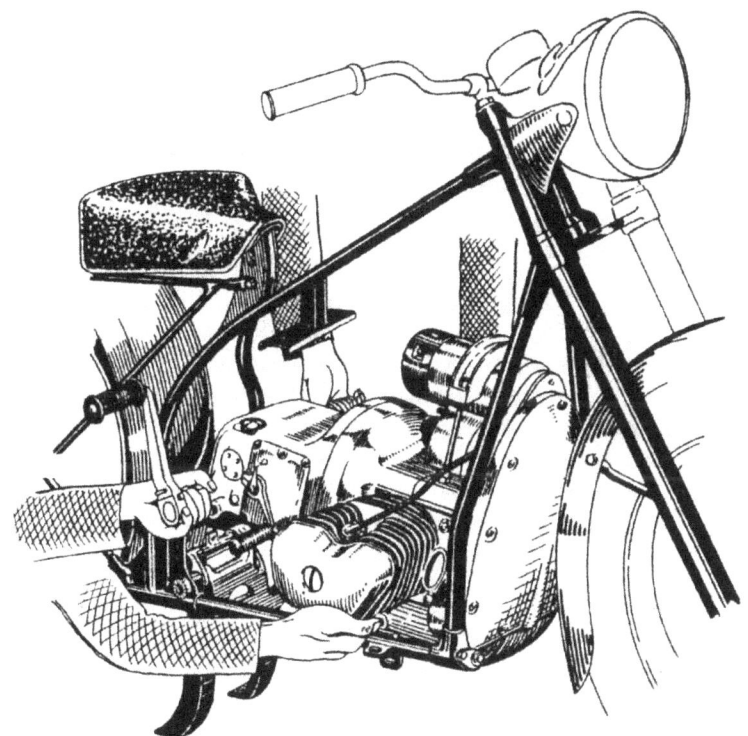

Fig. 9.   REMOVAL OF POWER UNIT FROM FRAME.

Separating Engine from Gearbox

Before commencing to separate the engine from the gearbox, drain off the gearbox oil as described in Section 3 'Lubrication,' page 15. These two units are held together by seven socket head screws, five long and two short, equally spaced around the periphery of the clutch housing. Unscrew these with the key provided in the tool kit. The gearbox can now be withdrawn from the engine.

REMOVAL OF CYLINDER HEADS AND CYLINDERS

Remove both sparking plugs, using a good fitting box spanner on the hexagon of the body and not on the smaller gland nut. Take off the rocker covers by unscrewing the centre screws (with their fibre washers) by the special tool (34/12). Revolve the flywheel until both the valves of the cylinder head being removed are on their seats. Remove the $\frac{1}{4}$" B.S.F. nut and washer from the underside of the push rod tunnel, and remove the 4—$\frac{3}{8}$" B.S.F. cylinder head nuts with their split washers. Lift off the head and remove the push rods, one at a time. These should now be labelled as described in Section 4 'Running Adjustments' page 28. Should the cylinder head resist removal do not use force but wait until the cylinder has been removed, then with the aid of a piece of wood in the bore, drift it off. Repeat procedure for the other cylinder head.

The cylinders are each retained by 6—$\frac{5}{16}$" B.S.F. nuts ($\frac{3}{8}$" B.S.F. on the Plus Series Models) situated around the base of the cylinder. One of these nuts is longer than the others and is fitted in the position adjacent to the clutch inspection cover plate or air funnel on the Plus Series models. When withdrawing the cylinders, the tappets (6/3) and the brass shims (6/2) should come away with the cylinders. Do not allow a piston to fall when it leaves the cylinder bore as this may cause damage.

The Plus Series machines may have several shims under each cylinder, these being .005" and .010" (.125 mm. and .250 mm.) thick. It is essential that they be replaced in the same order to maintain the correct compression ratio.

REMOVING PISTONS

Remove the circlips (7/3) from the pistons with pointed nose pliers, then drift out the gudgeon pins with the aid of a soft metal punch, supporting the piston and the connecting rod on the side opposite to that at which the force is being applied. Each piston should be scratch-marked on the inside top of the skirt so that its hand and position can be identified for re-assembly.

REMOVAL OF MAGDYNO UNIT FROM ENGINE

Unscrew the two special $\frac{1}{4}$" B.S.F. nuts on the bridge clamp (12/9) which is then free to lift off, after which the two long studs should be unscrewed from their sockets. Remove the two set bolts and washers securing the Magdyno flange to the crankcase. Lift the Magdyno off its platform, taking care not to damage the joint washer between the flange and the crankcase. Should it become necessary to remove the Magdyno pinion it is desirable to slacken the retaining nut prior to detaching the instrument from the crankcase. The special extractor **MUST** be used; any other method will damage the armature.

REMOVAL OF TIMING COVER AND GEARS

On the Standard models the timing cover is retained by 9—$\frac{1}{4}$" B.S.F. countersunk head setscrews. The removal of these allows the timing cover to be taken off, giving access to the timing gears. On the Plus Series models, there is a composite timing cover, one section of which forms the cover plate or holding plate for the revolution counter drive. Remove the cover plate first and note that the top setscrew also secures the timing cover to crankcase. The other retaining screws are of the socket head type and a key for these is provided in the tool kit.

Bend back the lock washers behind the crankshaft pinion nut and cam pinion bolts. Remove the crankshaft pinion nut and camshaft bolts, by 'scotching' the teeth of the gears with a soft metal wedge (a piece of $\frac{5}{16}$" diameter copper pipe is suitable).

To withdraw the Magdyno idler pinion, remove the split pin from the $\frac{7}{16}$" B.S.F. slotted nut and remove the nut, facing washer and pinion. The camshaft idler pinion is retained by a support plate (2/6) which is secured by a $\frac{7}{16}$" B.S.F. slotted nut (on the idler spindle) and 2—$\frac{1}{4}$" B.S.F. nuts with shakeproof washers. Remove the nuts, the support plate, its two distance tubes, and the idler pinion. With the extractor previously mentioned, withdraw the two cam pinions and remove the keys.

Pull off the crankshaft pinions and remove the oil retaining or distance washer (1/9) and key.

REMOVAL AND DISMANTLING OF FLYWHEEL CLUTCH

Remove the inspection cover (2/35) (or the air funnel on the Plus Series machines) which is situated immediately behind the left hand cylinder base; this gives access to the cable nipple which can be detached from the operating cam. Unscrew the cable adjuster bush (14/20) on top of the clutch bell housing and withdraw clutch control cable.

To remove the flywheel, withdraw the split pin and remove the flywheel nut (1/14) with a box spanner, holding the flywheel with the plate provided with the extractor. This plate should be secured by 2—$\frac{5}{16}$" B.S.F. screws to the crankcase (see Fig. 16). Use leverage in preference to hammering but if the latter has to be adopted, several light sharp blows will be better than one or two heavy concussive blows which might disturb the truth of the crankshaft. The flywheel and clutch assembly can now be pulled off, using the special extractor which can be obtained from the DOUGLAS Dealer or direct from the Factory Spares Department, and is illustrated in Fig. 16. Remove flywheel key (1/13). If it is considered necessary to dismantle the clutch, the six lock washers around the outer plate (13/1) will have to be bent back and each of the 6—$\frac{5}{16}$" B.S.F. nuts unscrewed progressively to release the spring pressure evenly. The pressure plate (13/11), complete with the six driving studs, their bushes (13/15) and shims (13/16) can now be withdrawn from the flywheel, thus separating flywheel, outer plate, driven plate with friction discs (on the Plus Series, cork inserts) and the six double clutch springs. Only if it is necessary for examination, should the operating cam (14/7) and the spigot assembly (14/6) be removed from the crankcase. The former is held by three small springs (14/18) and the spigot assembly by 3—$\frac{1}{4}$" B.S.F. nuts and split washers.

PARTING CRANKCASE

Remove the 4—$\frac{5}{16}$" B.S.F. nuts and washers inside the clutch bell housing, and the 3—$\frac{5}{16}$" B.S.F. nuts and washers on the front underside of the crankcase. With the connecting rods at T.D.C. and holding the crankcase by the timing section, allow a little clearance between the case and the work bench and gently tap the timing end of the crankshaft with a hide or rubber mallet, when the two portions should part. It is important, when carrying out this operation, not to allow the crankshaft and flywheel section to fall any distance as this will cause damage. As a further precaution, place a sack or pad of cloth on the bench beneath the crankcase.

The two camshafts can now be withdrawn from their bushes. To remove the crankshaft from the flywheel section of the crankcase, ensure that the connecting rods are at T.D.C. and support the case with the clutch housing uppermost and, allowing sufficient clearance between the shaft and the bench, knock out the crankshaft with the aid of a mallet or a hammer and soft drift. Here again, it is advisable to place a sack on the bench to avoid damaging the crankshaft. The ball bearing will probably come away with the crankshaft but if it does not, it can be drifted out of the crankcase.

On the early Mark III and Mark III Sports models, crankshaft end float is controlled by a flat location washer situated between the crankshaft pinion and the timing side main bush. On later models the control is effected by the use of .002", .005" or .010" (.051 mm., .128 mm. or .256 mm.) shims placed between the main ball bearing and the clutch cam spigot. Early series machines can be modified to adopt the shimming method of end float control by replacing the flat location washer by an oil retaining plate. The allowable end-float is between .005" and .008" (.128 mm. and .204 mm.). On the later Mark V models and Plus Series machines, the timing side main bush is fitted in two sections, each with its flange. In this case the flat thrust washer is re-introduced, dispensing with the shims, and the end-float is controlled by the manufacturing limits of the bush.

It is advisable upon removal of the crankshaft to tape the timing journal so as to prevent the entry of dirt, etc., into the oilways. Then carefully wrap the shaft in clean cloth and put it on one side.

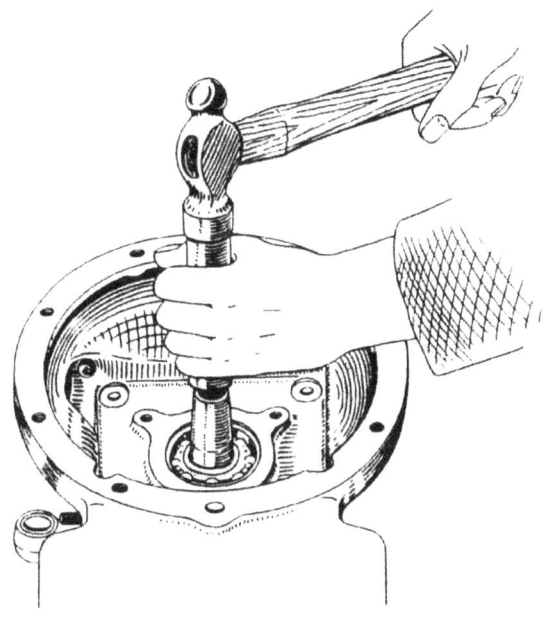

Fig. 10.   **REMOVAL OF CRANKSHAFT.**

REMOVAL OF OIL PUMP

The oil pump situated on the underside of the crankcase is retained by 3—¼" B.S.F. nuts and spring washers. Removal of these will permit the withdrawal of the cover plate and paper joint washer, leaving the oil pump body together with the cork joint washer, to be gently eased off its three studs. It is advisable at this point to replace the cover on the pump body, retaining this by three nuts and bolts, thus preventing the entry of dirt and the loss of the two vanes (4/7) and their spring.

DISMANTLING THE CYLINDER HEADS

Check the rockers for play in their bearings, as there is no necessity to dismantle these unless excessive play has developed. If it is necessary to remove the rocker bearing assembly with rockers, unscrew the 4—¼" B.S.F. nuts and remove the shakeproof washers. The bearing (cap and base) can now be parted and the rockers removed by unscrewing the 2—2 B.A. bolts (8/23) nuts and split washers. The valves can be removed without disturbing the rocker assembly; this operation calls for a valve spring compression tool as illustrated in Fig. 8. The valves, their springs, collars, cups (shim washers on the Plus Series) and collets should be segregated in order that they may be re-assembled in their original stations.

CRANKSHAFT

Check the connecting rods for slackness or roughness on the crankpin roller bearings. If for any reason the crankshaft has to be dismantled, it will be necessary to return the assembly to the Douglas dealer, who will supply a service exchange shaft. Check the connecting rods for alignment, by passing a gudgeon pin or straight bar of ⅝" (15.875 mm.) silver steel through the small ends of both rods. Check both main bearings for wear. Should the main ball bearing need renewing, it will have to be drawn off the crankshaft by an extractor tool and the new one fitted by a press to ensure that the crankshaft is not disturbed out of truth. It is important, also, to set the oil thrower (1/4) so that its two small holes are not shielded by the web of the crankshaft.

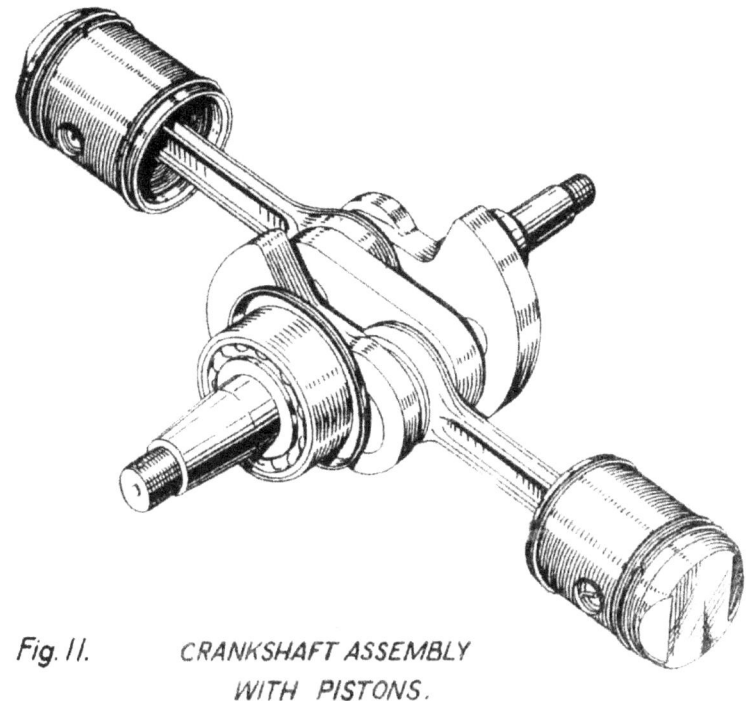

Fig. 11.   CRANKSHAFT ASSEMBLY
WITH PISTONS.

PISTONS

Examine:—

   Fit of the pistons on the gudgeon pins.
   Fit of the gudgeon pins in small end bushes.
   Pistons, for condition of skirts.
   Rings in grooves (up and down play).
   Ring gaps in cylinders. Rings should be carefully removed from the pistons for this and replaced in the same position.
   Note: **Max. gap, .012" or .3048 mm. New rings should have a gap of .006" or .1524 mm.**

CYLINDERS

If possible, check with the aid of a dial type cylinder gauge the cylinder bores, and if the diameter at any point throughout the length of the piston travel exceeds 2.404" (61 mm.), either new barrels will be required or the originals must be rebored and have over-sized pistons fitted.

MISCELLANEOUS

Check to ensure that all pinions are in good condition and that there is no sign of excessive wear on the teeth.

It is essential when rebuilding that every precaution be taken to ensure freedom from dirt and dust, as satisfactory operation is dependent on this. Immediately prior to rebuilding it is advisable to re-wash components, especially if there has been any lapse of time since the previous washing. During this final wash, all oil passages of the crankcase must be thoroughly syringed through. Have available a quantity of clean engine oil and give all bearings, pistons, etc., an initial coating of oil, also with the aid of a force feed oil can, squirt a quantity of oil into crankshaft oil passages.

Re-assembly

CRANKCASE

Before inserting the crankshaft into the flywheel section of the crankcase ensure that the main bearing ballrace is home on the crankshaft journal. Heat the crankcase in clean boiling water, place in position the shims (if they are used and if the clutch cam spigot has not been removed in dismantling) and insert the crankshaft ball bearing into its housing as far as possible. Have available

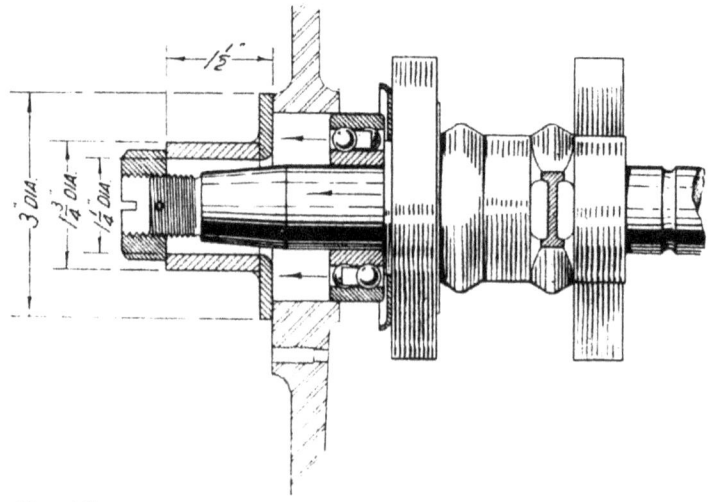

Fig. 12.   INSERTING FLYWHEEL SIDE OF CRANKSHAFT INTO CRANKCASE.

a tubular distance piece (Fig. 12) and draw in the crankshaft with the aid of the crankshaft flywheel nut. *Do not in any circumstances, attempt to force the crankshaft into the crankcase by hammering on the timing side end.* It is important when carrying out this operation that the connecting rods are at T.D.C. and correctly positioned in relation to their cylinder spigots—the right hand cylinder is offset forward—and that the connecting rods do not become jammed against the crankcase face.

Fit the camshafts into their respective bushes in the flywheel half of the crankcase ensuring that the camshaft with the pump worm is on the right hand side. Lightly smear the joint faces with a good quality jointing cement, taking care not to allow any to enter the drilled oil ways, and carefully place on new paper joints. The timing section of the crankcase can now be fitted, making sure that the connecting rods are clear of the crankcase halves, *i.e.* at T.D.C. and that the four drilled dowels register correctly. The crankcase assembly can now be secured by the 7—$\frac{5}{16}$" B.S.F. nuts and flat washers.

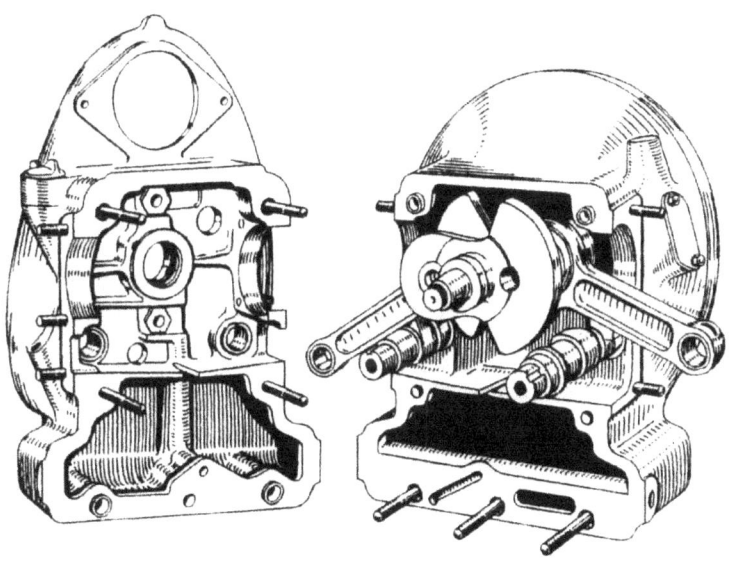

Fig. 13.   *CRANKCASE READY FOR ASSEMBLY.*

PISTONS AND CYLINDERS

Refit pistons, but take care to support the connecting rods when tapping in the gudgeon pins, for which a soft metal drift should be used. The pistons should be warmed, preferably in hot water, to ease the fitting of the gudgeon pins.

Fit new circlips to retain gudgeon pins, ensuring that they are correctly located in their grooves. It is essential that circlips are renewed after their original use. Place the brass shim (for the Plus Series models the several selective shims) on the cylinder and insert tappets into their housings. Fit the cylinder over the piston, easing

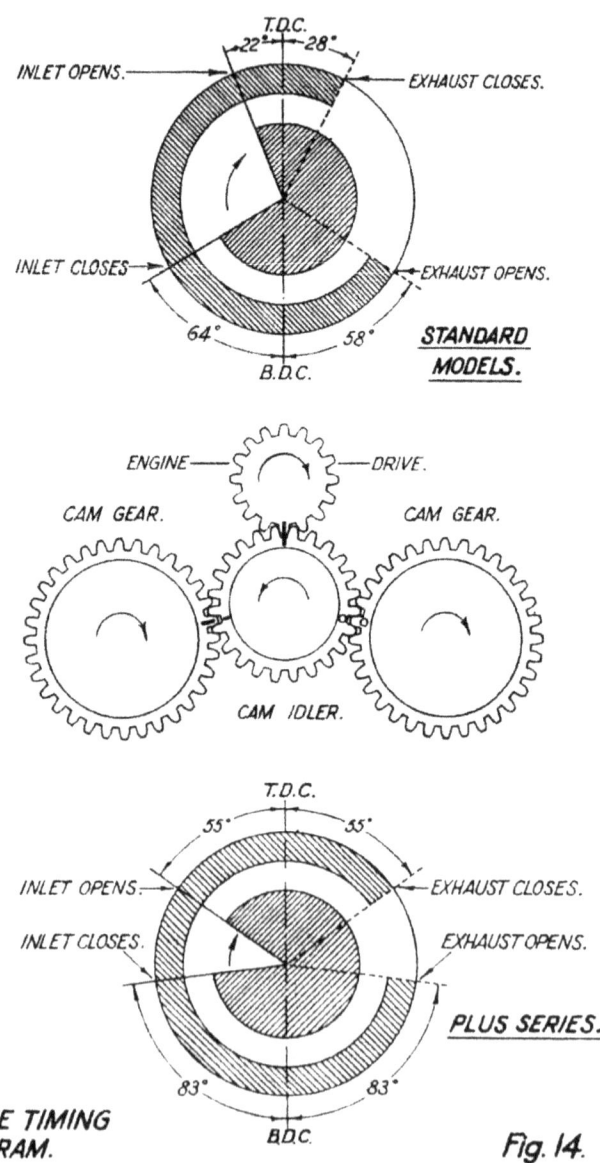

VALVE TIMING DIAGRAM.

Fig. 14.

each ring into the cylinder (use ring clamp if available). Secure with the six nuts and washers, taking note to replace special long nut on the left hand cylinder adjacent to the clutch inspection aperture.

REPLACEMENT OF VALVE TIMING GEARS

Place the oil retaining plate or location washer (1/9) over the timing end of the crankshaft and fit the key. Using a hollow drift, tap the cam drive pinion (1/8) (the one with fine teeth) on to the end of the crankshaft and make sure that the timing mark (see Fig. 14) is on the outside. Insert the parallel keys (3/8) into the camshafts and fit the cam pinions by tapping on, again ensuring that the timing marks are on the outside and the pinions fitted to their respective shafts. On the Plus Series models the pinions should be fitted to the camshafts before the crankcase halves are bolted together. In fitting these pinions the one with the 'line' timing mark (3/6) fits on the right hand shaft (facing the engine, left hand) and the one with the 'circle' timing mark (3/7) on the other shaft. Now place the camshaft idler pinion on its bush, so that it meshes with the two camshaft pinions and the crankshaft pinion. It is important that the timing marks on the teeth of the two camshaft pinions, the camshaft idler pinion, and the crankshaft pinion, are coincident. Fit the crankshaft pinion for the Magdyno drive and secure all pinions by their respective setscrews, nuts, tab washers and split pins. Do not forget to fit the two distance pieces (2/8) and to secure the camshaft idler pinion strap plate (2/6) by its 2—¼" B.S.F. nuts and shakeproof washers.

CYLINDER HEADS

Having ground in the valves refit them and the springs to the cylinder heads as instructed under decarbonisation, page 30. Refit rocker assembly if this has been dismantled. Put the rocker bearing base on its studs and fit rockers and the bearing cap. Secure with the 4—¼" B.S.F. nuts and shakeproof washers and the two small nuts, bolts (8/23) and split washers.

Insert the plain end of the push rods into the tappets, fit the cylinder head gasket, and put on the cylinder head. Make sure that the headed ends of the push rods locate in the rocker arm cups. Secure the cylinder head with the 4—⅜" B.S.F. nuts and split washers, and then the ¼" B.S.F. nut and washer beneath the push rod tunnel.

Oil Pump

Fit the cork joint washer so that the holes coincide with those of the pump (it is not an equilateral triangle) and then insert the oil pump, making sure that the oilways line up. Having checked that the two vanes and spring are ' in situ ' fit the paper washer between pump and cover plate and secure with the 3—¼" B.S.F. nuts and spring washers.

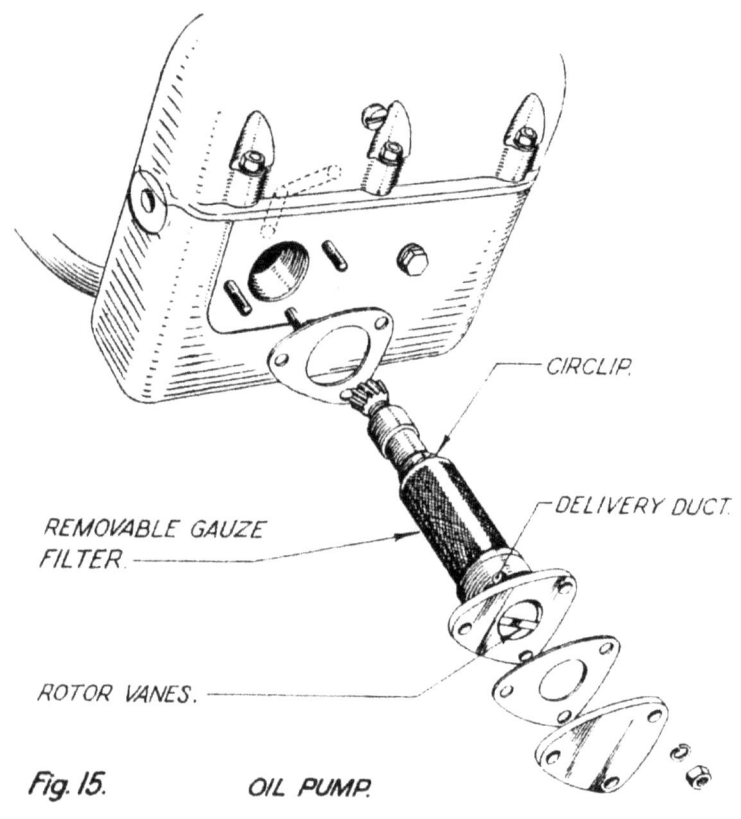

Fig. 15.   OIL PUMP.

Tappet Adjustment

Set the tappet clearances as previously instructed on page 19.

Ignition Timing

Before fitting the Magdyno, screw one magdyno clamp rod into the left hand position. Fit joint washer to flange and lower the magdyno unit on to its platform. Insert the two set bolts and tighten securely. Screw in the other clamp rod and after this has been secured fit the dynamo bridge clamp and tighten down.

The ignition timing is not marked on any model. It should be set with the contact breaker points just breaking when the pistons are 36° before top dead centre, and with magneto handlebar control lever set in the fully advanced position. When the magneto drive idler pinion (with its thrust washer between the pinion and the $\frac{7}{16}$" B.S.F. slotted nut) has been replaced, the magneto pinion can be placed on the armature spindle, care being taken that the spindle does not move whilst the nut is being screwed on finger tight. At this stage and again after finally tightening the nut, the timing should be re-checked to ensure that it has not slipped. A degree plate must be used for this operation and this can be attached to either the timing or flywheel end of the crankshaft. The accuracy necessary to achieve the correct magneto timing cannot be overstressed and, for this reason, piston movement down the cylinder cannot be relied upon as a means of measurement as any small build up of wear at many points could total several degrees (see Fig. 14).

To ensure that the correct cylinder is being timed, the valves should be on their seats with the corresponding brass segment of the magneto slip ring visible through the aperture made by removing the bakelite brush holder. The contact breaker points should be checked and adjusted if they are not set to .012" (.306 mm.)—a variation from this will alter the timing when, later, they are correctly adjusted. The bakelite brush holder can now be re-fitted and the sparking plugs, having been cleaned, can be replaced in the cylinder heads and the plug wires connected.

REPLACING TIMING COVER

Before replacing the timing cover, the breather situated in it should be examined to ensure that the disc valve is working freely. The Mark V models have a gauze baffle (5/2) in place of the valve assembly and this may be fitted to the earlier models with advantage.

The timing cover on the Standard and Competition models is retained by 9—$\frac{1}{4}$" B.S.F. countersunk screws, and that on the Plus Series models by eight socket headed set screws and one hexagon setscrew, which also retains the cover plate for the gearbox of the revolution counter.

The paper joint for the timing cover must always be renewed and a smear of good quality jointing cement may be used on both faces.

FLYWHEEL CLUTCH

If the clutch operating cam spigot (14/6) has been removed, replace with the 3—$\frac{1}{4}$" B.S.F. nuts and spring washers, and replace the crankshaft shims (1/12) (if used). Insert the clutch cam assembly and attach by the 3 springs. Fit the control cable into the clutch housing, coupling the nipple to the operating arm. To assemble the clutch lay the pressure plate (13/11) on the bench with the 6 driving pins uppermost and place on the driven plate with its splined boss (13/9) downwards. Fit the flywheel over the driving pins,

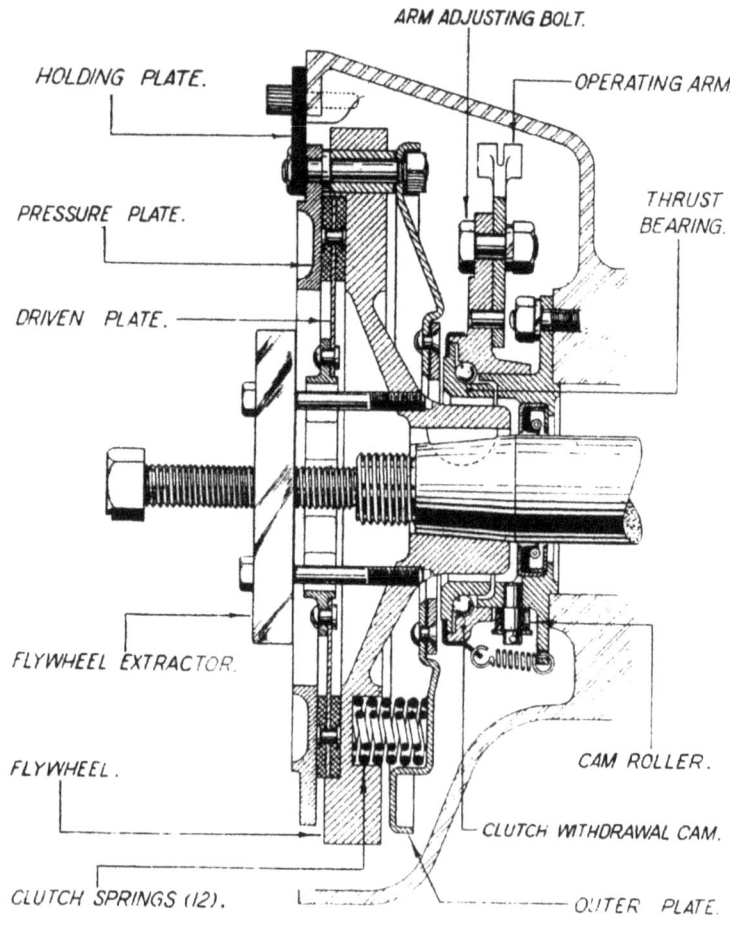

Fig. 16.   CLUTCH ASSEMBLY SHOWING EXTRACTOR AND HOLDING PLATE.

making sure that the line mark on the periphery is coincident with that on the pressure plate. Place the twelve (six pairs) springs in the housings in the flywheel and the six shim washers (13/16) on the driving pins. Locate the outer plate over the driving pins, again ensuring that the index mark registers with those on the other two components.

With the aid of a suitable clamp (this can be made from two strips of steel, a long bolt and nut) the assembly can be compressed and the six nuts and lock washers fitted.

Fit the woodruff key in the crankshaft, ensuring that there is no side play. If for any reason a new key is used, care must be taken to see that there is a slight clearance between the top of the key and the flywheel key way. The whole clutch assembly should now be fitted to the crankshaft. 'Scotch' the flywheel as previously described and tighten up the flywheel nut, using leverage rather than the hammer.

Lock with the split pin.

Dismantling of Gearbox

Withdraw the cotter pin, which is secured by a $\frac{1}{4}$" B.S.F. nut, and remove the kickstart lever and spring. Remove the footchange pedal and cover, taking out the six socket headed screws, when it will be possible to proceed with dismantling the remainder of the selector mechanism.

Remove the selector spindle retaining plug (17/2), situated in the gearbox cover plate in the bell housing, and withdraw the spindle (17/1) using a $\frac{3}{16}$" B.S.F. bolt and a piece of tube as a drawbolt—the end of the spindle is drilled and tapped. Remove the selector forks, lifting the front one to clear the spring and plunger, which should also be removed. To remove the shock-absorber unit; lock the gear train by sliding the pinions to engage two gears simultaneously. Remove the split pin and nut, leaving the shock-absorber components free to be withdrawn from the splined sleeve (19/15) on the final drive spindle; the sleeve will remain attached to the spindle. With the peg spanner provided (34/12) unscrew the duralumin plug at the other side of the gearbox and, using a drift of soft material, tap the final drive spindle through from the sprocket end and withdraw it from the opening made by removing the duralumin cap.

It will be seen that as the spindle is being tapped out, the splined sleeve is left behind, and when the spindle has passed completely through, this sleeve is free to be lifted from its engagement with the hollow shaft to which it is tongued.

Unscrew the 8—¼" B.S.F. nuts (two of which secure the shock-absorber cover), and remove the final drive bevel gear and housing complete, taking care not to damage the brass shims and joint faces of the housing and gearbox case.

Unscrew the ½" B.S.F. nut (18/11) and washer on the spindle situated below the kickstarter bush and a little forward of it. After slackening the locknut, use a screwdriver to partially withdraw the locking screw (15/16) from under the gearbox case. The spindle must now be tapped into the case from this end until it lies approximately ¾" in from the face of the boss. The spindle runs through a hollow shaft, (18/6) the end of which can now be seen, and this hollow shaft has a slot milled in it. Using a screwdriver inserted in this slot, rotate the shaft approximately one quarter of a turn. Looking into the box from the kickstarter side it will be seen that the kickstarter mechanism comprises a worm bush (18/7) which is free on the hollow shaft previously mentioned. On the worm bush rides a small spur gear pinion (18/8) which engages with the larger pinion on the kickstarter spindle (18/13). On the inner face of the small pinion are cut dog teeth which, when the pinion rides forward on the worm bush, engage with the teeth on the bevel gear (18/5) and this in turn drives the small bevel (16/31) on the end of the layshaft. The end of the worm bush and pinion is spring loaded so that it is held forward against the shoulder of the hollow shaft.

With the hollow shaft turned as directed above, apply pressure to the large bevel pinion through the final drive aperture. This will ensure that the hollow shaft is hard against the internal shoulder of the boss. With pressure maintained screw up the locking screw to retain the hollow shaft in position.

The spindle may now be finally driven out, preferably with a ⅜" diameter (9.5 mm.) drift which will thread the large bevel gear with its bearing bush (18/3) and thrust washers (18/2 and 18/4) and maintain them in correct sequence for removal.

Bend back the tabs of the lock washer and with the spindle held in a vice, remove the nut securing the kickstart pinion to the shaft (18/13). Drift the shaft out of the gear, taking care not to bruise the threads; the gear can then be extracted from the box.

To complete the dismantling of the kickstart mechanism, release the locking screw. This will allow the hollow shaft (complete with worm bush, pinion, washer and spring) to be withdrawn.

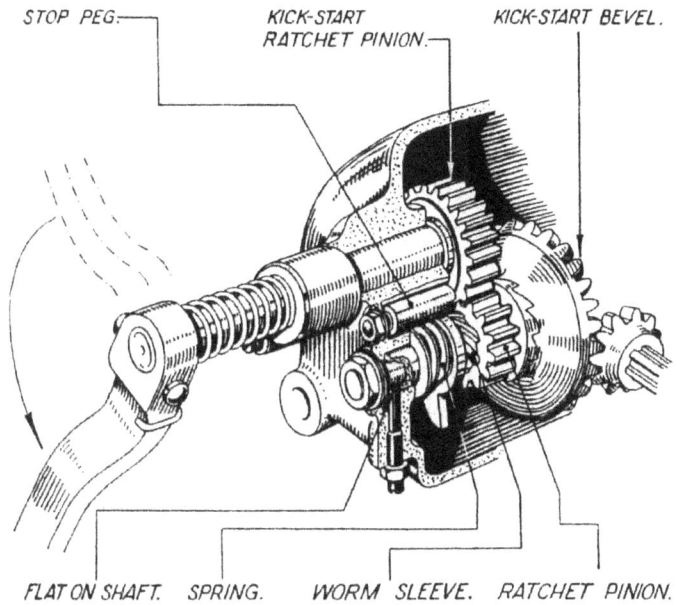

Fig. 17. KICK-START. SECTIONAL VIEW.

REMOVAL OF SHAFTS AND GEARS

The bevel gears at the ends of the mainshaft and layshaft are now accessible. The tabs of the lock washers should be tapped back, and the nuts removed, the gear train being first locked as previously described. The layshaft bevel gear can now be removed with the aid of a small pinch bar, but the gear (16/19) on the mainshaft requires special attention; this is dealt with later.

If it is considered necessary to examine the main shaft roller bearing, the splined coupling (16/1) should be removed at this stage, as it is a difficult operation when the train of gears is out of the box. To remove the splined coupling, lock the gear train and remove the large hexagon nut, using a good fitting box spanner. With the aid of an extractor the coupling can now be removed. Care should be exercised to prevent damage to the oil spinner mounted upon the coupling.

Note:—The centre bolt of the extractor should not bear directly on the end of the sleeve pinion but a suitable distance piece should be employed.

Unscrew the 6—¼" B.S.F. nuts and split washers holding the cover (15/2) at the front end of the case; the layshaft, mainshaft and gears are now ready to be withdrawn.

Support the bell housing of the gearcase on two stout pieces of wood, allowing clearance for the subsequent withdrawal of the gearbox end cover. To remove the gearbox end cover together with the gear train it is necessary to tap the end of the mainshaft (which has had its nut refitted to prevent bruising of the thread) using a hammer and drift. A few sharp blows should be sufficient to release the assembly, comprising shafts, gears and cover, leaving behind the mainshaft bevel gear which is a press fit in the bearing. The bevel gear may be released by several light taps on a long drift inserted from the front of the case. The box is now completely dismantled with the exception of the sub-assemblies and the bearing retaining plate.

To complete the dismantling of the mainshaft, withdraw this with its bush (or needle rollers on the Plus Series machines) from the sleeve pinion (16/8). The two sliding gears can then be drawn off their splines. The large gear (26/14) (and the needle rollers on the Plus Series machines) together with spacing washer at the final drive end can also be withdrawn. The bronze bush on the Standard models (or hardened steel sleeve on the Plus Series models) and the inner thrust washer remain on the mainshaft and can be removed by an extractor, placed over the thrust washer.

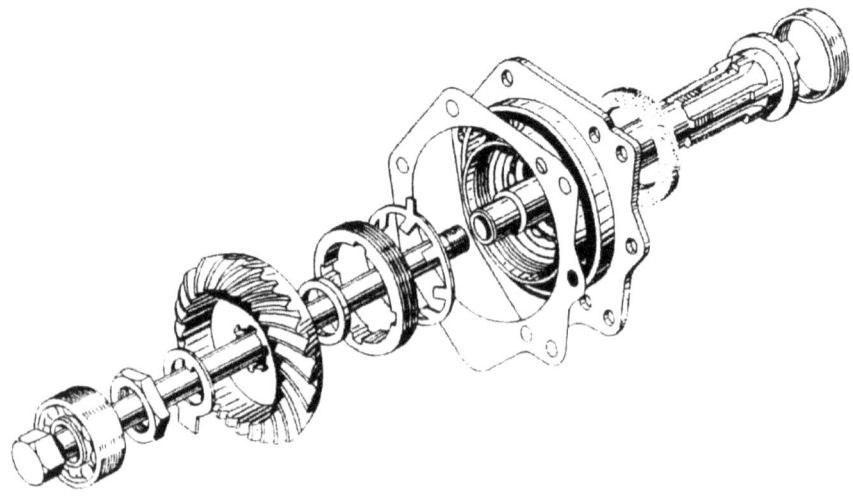

To dismantle the layshaft, first revolve the sleeve pinion until the flat machined in the oil thrower (16/9) is linable with the layshaft ball bearing. The layshaft with its ball bearing may now be withdrawn from the end cover, after which the two end gears may be drawn off and the two sliding gears removed.

If the splined coupling has been removed as previously described, access to the sleeve pinion roller bearing can now be obtained by

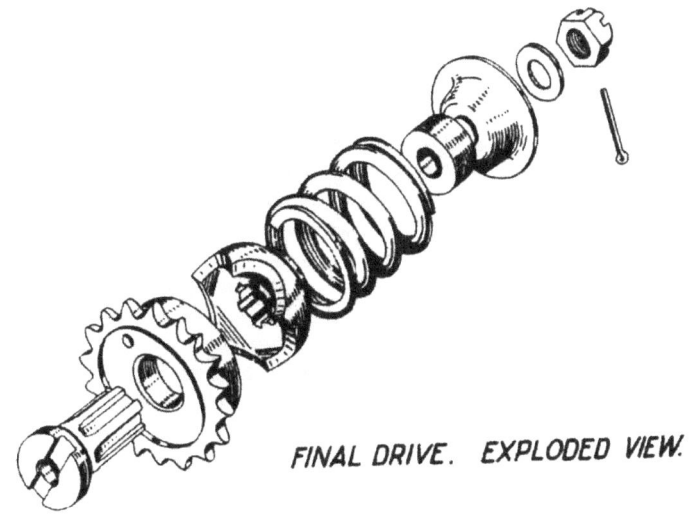

FINAL DRIVE. EXPLODED VIEW.

Fig. 18.

removing the countersunk headed screws securing the bearing retaining plate (16/6). The shaft complete with spinner, bearing rollers and felt oil seal, should now be drawn out of the gearbox end cover.

To replace either the main or layshaft rear bearings it is necessary to remove the bearing retaining plate (16/34) by unscrewing the countersunk screws.

FINAL DRIVE

To dismantle the final drive unit (when this is removed from the gearbox) bend back the tabs of the lock washer and unscrew the nut (19/4) securing the bevel gear to the hollow shaft. To do this, replace the splined sleeve and final drive bolt, using a distance piece to compensate for the components not included. Hold the splined sleeve in a vice with soft jaws (or use copper clamps). With the nut removed draw the bevel gear off its splines, and remove the distance

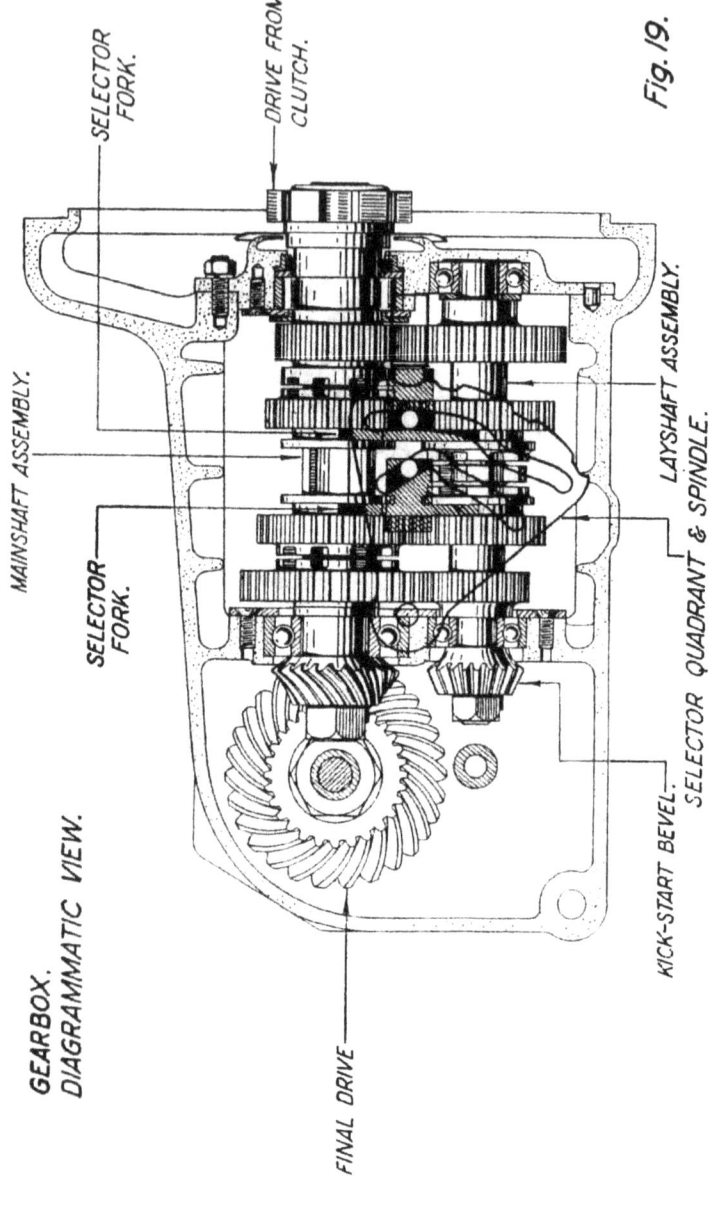

Fig. 19.

GEARBOX. DIAGRAMMATIC VIEW.

piece situated between the ball race and bevel gear, after which the shaft is free to be pushed out of the bearing. If it is necessary to extract the ball bearing, unscrew the large ring nut (19/8) which becomes visible after removing the bevel gear. The bearing can now be taken out.

If at any time the felt oil seal ring needs renewing, it will be necessary to dismantle the final drive unit as far as the removal of the hollow shaft. Care must be taken to avoid cutting the felt washer when the sleeve is re-assembled.

Re-assembly of Gearbox

Treat the dismantled components in a similar manner to those of the engine unit, *i.e.* wash off thoroughly, and examine for any signs of wear. Renew where necessary.

When re-assembling give all components an initial supply of oil.

If new bearings have been fitted to the rear end of the gearbox, replace the bearing retaining plate and secure with countersunk screws, corking the plate into the screw slots.

To re-assemble the final drive unit, insert the bearing in its housing, and secure with the large ring nut and lock washer. Insert the hollow spindle and press home into the bearing with the dogs facing outwards and with the oil seal sleeve tube in position. Place the distance piece over the shaft, and press the bevel gear onto the splines, securing it with the hexagon nut and tab washer.

To assemble the layshaft, place on the sliding gears, ensuring that the larger diameter gear is to the front portion of the shaft. Insert the two woodruff keys at either end of the shaft and press on the gears with the boss of each outermost. Fit the distance washer (16/24) and press home the front ball bearing.

RE-ASSEMBLY OF SLEEVE GEAR PINION AND LAYSHAFT INTO COVER

Ensure that the oil seal is in position. Place the spinner on the shaft with the lip facing forward and fit the bearing retaining plate. Apply a liberal quantity of good quality vaseline to the roller track, then around the track of the shaft place the $18-\frac{1}{4}''$ diameter rollers. Push home the shaft, complete with rollers, spinner and retaining plate. A useful method for entering the bearing rollers into their outer track is to fit an elastic band around the row of rollers, cutting this band to facilitate its removal when the rollers have entered. The layshaft assembly should now be fitted to the cover.

Thread the sliding gears on to the mainshaft, with their dogs outermost, and the larger gear to the rear. Insert the front end of the mainshaft, with its bronze bush, into the sleeve gear pinion. (On the Plus Series 48 needle rollers are used, instead of the bronze bush).

Fit on the large low gear pinion, at the rear of the shaft, with its dogs facing inwards. Fit the outside thrust washer with its oil slots against the gear. (On the Plus Series the thrust washer is not slotted, and the gear is fitted with 33 needle rollers).

Fit the mainshaft bevel to its bearing. To do this it may be necessary to use a draw bolt, which is simply a long threaded bolt, with a suitably large washer at either end, and nut.

Replace the front cover assembly comprising the mainshaft and layshaft units, taking care that the joint washer (15/3) has been fitted to the cover and that the two shafts enter their respective locations. It may be necessary to drift the mainshaft home into its bevel gear. Secure the cover with the 6—$\frac{1}{4}$" B.S.F. nuts and spring washers. Insert the key into the driving shaft and fit on the splined coupling, securing it with the large hexagon nut. This nut should be tightened with the aid of a box spanner, whilst the gears are locked in the manner already described. With the shaft still locked, press on the layshaft bevel gear and fasten both this and the mainshaft bevel with the tab washers and nuts.

RE-ASSEMBLY OF KICKSTART MECHANISM

To re-assemble the kickstart mechanism the following procedure should be followed:—

Fit the ratchet pinion to the worm bush and slide these on to the hollow spindle with the ratchet teeth against the conical end of the hollow spindle. Fit the spring and then the flat washer. (Certain early Mark III models may be fitted with a two coil spring—if so this should be replaced by the three coil type). This assembly can now be inserted into the hole in the gearcase, working through the final drive aperture. Press the assembly home, setting the stop of the worm bush against the stop pin which has remained held in the gearcase. Whilst the assembly is held in the pressed in position screw in the locking screw so that it contacts the hollow spindle— but does not pass into the slot; this will retain the location against the action of the spring. Fit the kickstart lever spindle with its key in position and press or tap on the 20T pinion.

The engagement of the teeth on this pinion with those of the ratchet pinion will determine the angular position of the kickstart pedal. Since the ratchet pinion is free to be removed and re-stationed upon the worm, the final positioning of the kickstart lever can be ascertained. The flat on the spindle for the cotter pin should be in line with the centre of the bore for the final drive shaft. The $\frac{7}{16}$" B.S.F. nut and lock washer, retaining the 20T pinion, can now be fitted, the nut being finally tightened in the fashion previously described.

REPLACEMENT OF KICKSTART BEVEL GEAR

The kickstart bevel gear bush and outer washer should now be threaded into position, the teeth meshing with the layshaft bevel gear.

The inner and outer washers are identical on models up to the Mark IV, but the Mark V, 80 Plus and 90 Plus models have a thicker outer washer. The outer washer is the one between the hollow spindle and the bush and can be identified as it is .156" (39.6 mm.) thick whilst the inner washer is .116" (29.5 mm.) thick.

The operation of fitting in these parts requires special care to make sure that the outer washer does not fall out of position, and it is recommended that the gearbox be laid on its side with the final drive aperture uppermost. Place the inner washer on the spindle, with its chamfered bore face towards the larger diameter of the spindle. Tap the spindle until the threaded end is approximately 1" from the face of the boss. Loosen the locking screw which has been temporarily securing the hollow shaft in position. The slot of the hollow shaft should still be visible when looking into the boss, and with the aid of a screwdriver inserted in the slot the hollow shaft should be rotated until the slot registers with the locking screw hole.

Drive the spindle through, ensuring that its flat also registers with the locking screw hole and slot in the shaft. The locking screw should now be screwed home, but should not be finally tightened until the spindle has been secured in position with its $\frac{7}{16}$" B.S.F. nut and washer. Lock up the locking screw with its $\frac{5}{16}$" nut.

HOUSING ASSEMBLY

Fit the final drive bevel and housing assembly into position in the box, replacing the same number of shims as found when dismantling. When driving the hollow shaft into the ball bearing on the kickstart side of the box, care must be taken to ensure that the shaft enters the ball bearing squarely, and that the teeth of the bevels are in mesh.

Secure the assembly in position with the 8—$\frac{1}{4}$" B.S.F. nuts and insert the final drive spindle from the kickstart side, if necessary gently tapping home until the hexagon head rests against the bearing.

Press on the splined shaft at the shock-absorber end of spindle so that the slot mates with the dogs in the hollow spindle; if necessary tap home gently before placing on the sprocket with its cam lobes facing outwards. Push the shock-absorber cam on to the splines so that the lobes mate with the sprocket. The assembly of this section should be completed by placing on the distance piece, spring and end cap, securing these with the $\frac{1}{2}$" B.S.F. nut, washer and split pin.

RE-ASSEMBLING SELECTOR MECHANISM

The plunger, spring, selector forks and supporting spindle can now be fitted. Note that the driving pins of the forks are fitted facing each other and the actual forks locate in the annular grooves of the sliding pinions. The forks can be identified by the fact that the front fork (third and top gears) has its driving pin nearly in line with the fork but in the case of the rear fork (first and second gears) the driving pin is well off centre. Tap home the selector spindle and finally locate it by screwing tight the aluminium plug. To lock the plug, it is advisable to lightly cork the metal of the cover plate to the screwdriver slot of the plug.

The aluminium cap at the kickstarter end of the final drive spindle can now be replaced and secured with the aid of the peg spanner.

Rejoining Engine and Gearbox

Before proceeding any farther with the assembly of the gearbox it is necessary to bolt the engine and gearbox units together.

Lay the engine unit on the bench, resting on the timing cover, and centralise the clutch plate by disengaging the clutch (through the clutch inspection housing). Gently lower the gearbox on to the engine unit so that the splined coupling on the gearbox sleeve pinion mates up with the splined boss of the clutch plate. Press home the gearbox into the spigot of the bell housing and insert the seven socket head screws, noting that the two shorter ones are fitted on the left side. Tighten these gradually, working around until they are all quite tight.

GEARCHANGE MECHANISM

The gearchange mechanism should now be added, but before so doing it is necessary to remove the selector quadrant (17/5) from the assembly, as this must be located separately. To do this, remove the neutral indicator (except on Mark III models) and carefully pull off the selector quadrant, which is secured by a parallel key and should withdraw fairly easily. The selector quadrant should now be fitted to the gearbox and the gear selected for this should be neutral. There are several indentations in the edge of the quadrant and neutral gear is the second indentation from the bottom. Engage the quadrant spindle into its bush in the gearbox but before pressing it right home it is necessary to lift the gear location plunger (17/8) which is spring loaded. This can be done by levering with a screwdriver. The quadrant can now be fully engaged, but it is necessary to ensure that the selector fork driving pins engage with the cam tracks in the quadrant. Fit the gear change cover, making sure that the spring (17/7) on the outside spindle of the quadrant does not become detached and that the joint washer (15/21) is in correct position. Secure the cover with the six socket head screws. Fit the gearchange pedal with its felt washer, and the kickstart lever.

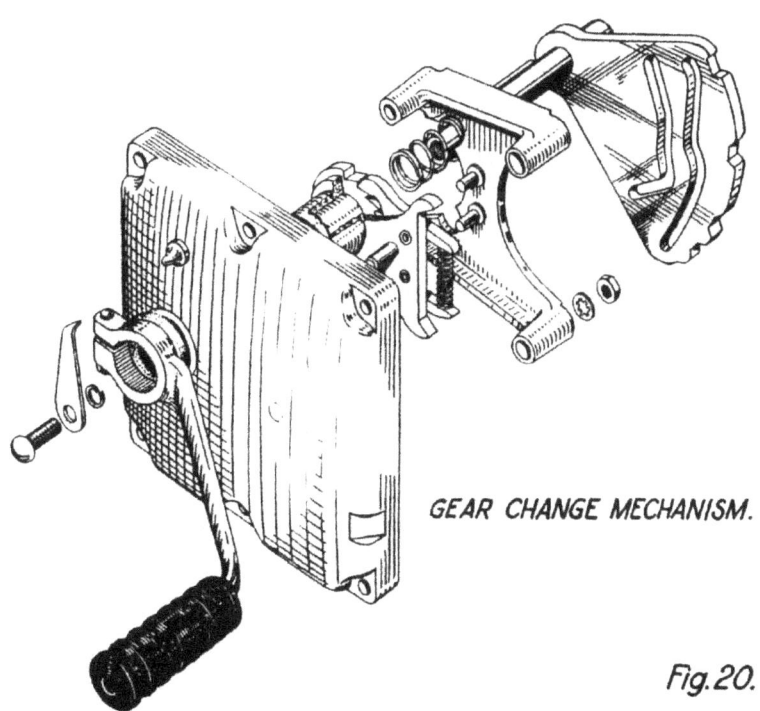

GEAR CHANGE MECHANISM.

Fig. 20.

Replacement of Engine—Gearbox Unit in Frame

The complete unit is now ready for replacement in the frame, and this should be done in the following manner:—Working from the right hand side of the machine insert the unit diagonally, locating the timing cover between the frame down tubes. Now lift the rear portion of the gearbox so that it will clear the pivot point of the rear suspension, and when it is within the confines of the frame, lower the gearbox into position. Before installing the power unit a block of suitable height should be placed between the bottom frame members to take the weight of the engine and gearbox until the mounting bolts have been fitted. The front mounting bolt, with its two spacing washers, should be fitted first and the nut and washer screwed on, but not finally secured. The rear mounting bolt, which also has the right side footrest attached, should then be inserted, ensuring that the distance pieces and shim washers are fitted in correct sequence at both sides of the gearbox and that they are a 'snug' fit. Fit left side footrest and after adjusting for position, secure the assembly with the nut. The front mounting bolt should now be finally tightened. The Plus Series machines have adjustable distance pieces which should not be varied beyond ensuring that the gearbox becomes a 'snug' fit in the frame. The Competition model gearbox is supported between two lugs mounted upon the saddle tubes and distance pieces are not used.

Final Re-assembly

Fit the exhaust pipes, making sure that they are well home in the exhaust ports. On the Mark III and IV models with the single cast silencer under the gearbox, 2—$\frac{5}{16}$" B.S.F. set bolts, with flat and split washers, retain the pipes to lugs on the bottom frame tubes. The same bolts secure the crash bars, when fitted. These bolts, together with the nuts securing the silencer clips, should be well tightened. The clips between the pipes and the cylinders on the Mark III Sports and the clips holding the pipes to the bottom frame tubes on the Mark IV Sports and the Mark V should also be well secured. The Plus Series exhaust system is similar to the Mark V but the pipes are held into the ports by gland nuts, C and A washers being used between the flange on the pipe and the port.

Thread on the chain and secure as previously detailed then fit the shock-absorber cover and secure by 2—$\frac{1}{4}$" B.S.F. nuts and split washers.

Replace accumulator carrier and secure with the 4—$\frac{1}{4}$" B.S.F. setscrews and split washers. On the Mark IV and Mark V models, the two distance pieces must be fitted between the bottom of the carrier and the gearbox. If fitted, the air cleaner bracket is also secured by the two top set screws.

Hook the short neck of the stand spring on to the accumulator carrier.

With the aid of a piece of twine, tension the spring and hook the long neck on to the stand.

On the Mark III model only, the tool box, which is located under the saddle, should now be re-fitted (using the two reinforcing strips) and secured by the 4—$\frac{1}{4}$" B.S.F. nuts and bolts. Replace the automatic voltage control unit, securing this with the fixing strap, and bolt this unit to the toolbox. Replace the accumulator connecting the positive and negative leads to their sockets, and slide over the rubber sleeves which are threaded on to the wires. Replace the contact breaker cover with the earth button lead. Connect the two remaining earthing leads to the Magdyno body by the grub screw and fit the two dynamo wires. Check the wiring of the electrical system by switching on the lights and operating the horn. Should the ammeter register on the 'charge side,' it is an indication that the accumulator leads are crossed.

Re-fit the carburettors (float chambers inwards), ensuring that the joint washers are in good condition, as any air leak seriously effects the performance of the machine. Should an air leak be detected, replace the joint and, with a straight edge, check the flange of the carburettor. If this is distorted, it can be filed flat but care must be taken to ensure that the swarf does not enter the carburettor. Replace the carburettor controls, taking care that the needles and slides are not damaged and are seating correctly. Secure with the knurled ring nuts. Replace the air cleaner unit (if fitted) and ensure that the metal seating washers are fitted between the carburettors and the rubber seals.

Before fitting the petrol tank this should be examined internally, and if necessary any dirt or foreign matter cleaned out. Place the tank over the top frame tubes, position, then feed through the front retaining bolt—on the Mark III and the Mark III Sports models it is $\frac{5}{16}$" B.S.F. but on the later models a $\frac{1}{4}$" B.S.F. bolt which passes through a rubber sleeve in the head lug. On the Mark IV models onwards the tank provides three alternative stations at this fixing point. These stations, together with the series of holes provided in the knee grip plates, allow a variable location of the knee grips to afford the most comfortable riding position. Before tightening the nut on the retaining bolt, screw in the two rear fixing setscrews and tighten without using excessive force, making sure that the rubber and fibre washers and the voltage control bracket are interposed between tank and support. (It is important at this stage to ensure that the tank does not touch the frame other than at its anchorage points). The setscrews should now be wired together, through their drilled heads, and the front bridge strap fitted by the 2—$\frac{5}{16}$" B.S.F. setscrews with flat and split washers.

Connect petrol feed pipe(s) to the tank and float chambers. Anchor the saddle at the nose, inserting the bolt in the right hand side, where the saddle seat has been lifted for this purpose, and secure with the locknut.

A FINAL CHECK OVER OF THE INSTALLATION OF THE POWER UNIT SHOULD BE MADE BEFORE PROCEEDING FURTHER.

RESTARTING AFTER OVERHAUL

Fill engine sump and gearbox with correct grade of lubricant, remove machine from trestle, flood carburettors and start the machine. Do not ' rev ' the engine but allow it to run at a moderate speed. When on the road a modified running-in procedure should be adopted depending on the nature and amount of parts renewed.

Rear Suspension

On the spring frame models the duplex frame follows normal layout. From the steering head, splayed twin down tubes are taken to the forward ends of the parallel horizontal frame tubes which form the support for the Engine—Gearbox Unit. Another pair of tubes from the top of the head lug slope backwards and then curve downwards and are attached to the bottom tubes by special lugs. The tubes are brazed at all lug joints.

In addition to supporting the engine—gearbox unit the parallel lower frame tubes form an integral part of the rear suspension system. Inside each tube and running throughout its entire length is a torsion bar (20/23) of special spring steel. The torsion bars are splined at each end, the front end being secured to the main frame by anchorage brackets (20/24) and the rear end projecting beyond the end of the bottom frame members. Mounted on the splines at the rear end of each bar is a forked lever (20/28) in which is secured one end of a connecting link (20/37) riding on a ball type trunnion. The top end of the link is attached to the rear wheel fork, the actual point of attachment being in the underside of the channel section. The forked levers at the ends of the torsion bars, supported on the ends of the main frame tubes, ride on phosphor bronze bushes. The rear fork pivot pins (20/18) are mounted on the vertical portion of the special frame lugs situated behind the gearbox. The lugs of the rear fork house phosphor bronze bushes in which the pivot pins operate. The hinge points are so positioned in relation to the final drive sprocket that variation in chain length over the maximum fork movement is negligible.

The operation of the Douglas rear springing is very simple and can be described as follows. The weight of the machine and rider is transmitted *via* the linkage to the torsion bars, effecting a given amount of twist. Increase in the load, such as occurs when the wheel strikes a bump, imparts more twist to the bars. As the bars are anchored at the front, the twist is absorbed by the spring steel from which they are made. After passing over the bump the resilience of the steel reverses the twist and causes the wheel to revert to its normal position. The effect of this action is that the wheel follows the undulations in the road surface without imparting vertical movement to the machine. This special torsion bar suspension is fitted to all models excepting the Competition model, which has a rigid type frame.

REMOVAL OF REAR FORK AND TORSION BARS

Throughout the life of the machine the rear suspension system will require very little attention other than regular greasing. Should it be necessary at any time to dismantle the rear springing the following procedure should be adopted:—

Remove the rear wheel in the manner previously described and disconnect the bottom joints of the connecting links where they attach to the forked levers of the torsion bars. To do this remove the $2-\frac{7}{16}''$ B.S.F. nuts and bolts (20/38), taking care not to lose the four cupped washers (20/39 and 20/40) when each bolt is withdrawn. Before removing the pivot pins on which the rear fork hinges, it is necessary to knock out (by drifting from the underside) the two Mills locking pins (20/19) situated on the outside and to the rear of

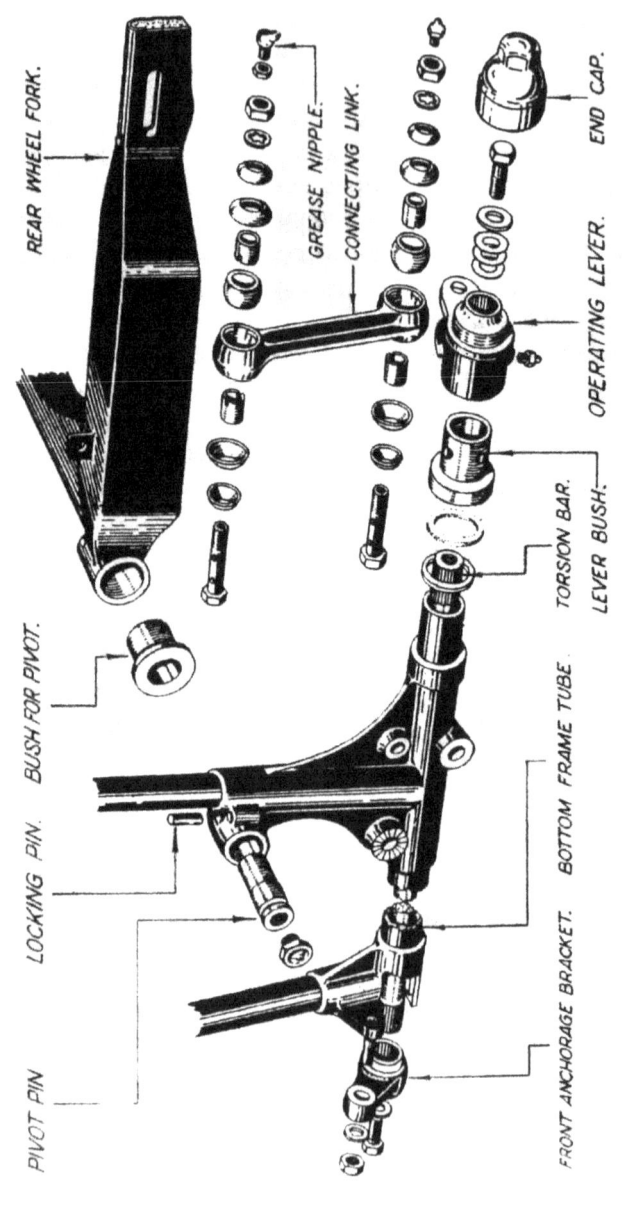

Fig. 21. REAR SUSPENSION. EXPLODED VIEW.

the pivot pin housings. After these have been extracted the end caps with greaser nipples (20/21) should be removed from the pivot pins, and the threads in the pins used for extraction purposes with the aid of a suitable bolt ($\frac{1}{2}''$ B.S.F.) and distance tube. Remove the pivot pins. The rear fork, complete with the 2 links and the distance washer (20/20) on the right hand side, is now free to be withdrawn from the frame.

The links themselves can be removed from the rear fork by extracting the 2—$\frac{7}{16}''$ B.S.F. nuts and bolts which retain them in their housings inside each fork member. Care must be taken not to lose the cupped washers when the bolts are withdrawn. The ball joint (20/42) and sleeves (20/41) from the ends of each link can now be removed for examination.

Remove from the torsion bar levers the aluminium end caps (20/36) which are secured by a fine thread. Unscrew the retaining bolts (20/34), remove packing shims, and withdraw the forked levers from the splined ends of the torsion bars.

Remove the nuts securing the anchorage brackets of the torsion bars at the front end of the bottom frame tube and withdraw from the frame the torsion bars complete with brackets.

When the torsion bars are out of the frame great care must be taken to avoid any damage such as bruising or bending, and the grease must not be removed from the bars unless *absolutely necessary*. If at any time the surfaces of the torsion bars become corroded or damaged renewal is necessary as a fatigue failure will ultimately occur.

RE-ASSEMBLY OF TORSION BARS AND REAR FORK

Examine all components before commencing to re-assemble, and obtain new ones where necessary.

The torsion bars are handed and it is essential that they be re-fitted correctly with the painted ends towards the front of the machine. Originally, the left hand bar was painted with a red band, but later and currently it is marked yellow. The right hand bar was and is still marked green. It will be appreciated that the fitting of one new bar only would unbalance the suspension system and for that reason we offer torsion bars only in balanced pairs.

Ensure that the torsion bars are adequately greased or vaselined for protection against corrosion, and insert them in the bottom frame tubes. Secure the brackets with the 2—$\frac{3}{8}''$ B.S.F. nuts and washers. The forked levers, complete with the bronze bushes and felt seal rings, should now be fitted to the torsion bars and frame with the greaser nipples pointing downwards. In the unloaded position the forked levers should lie at an angle of 30½° below the

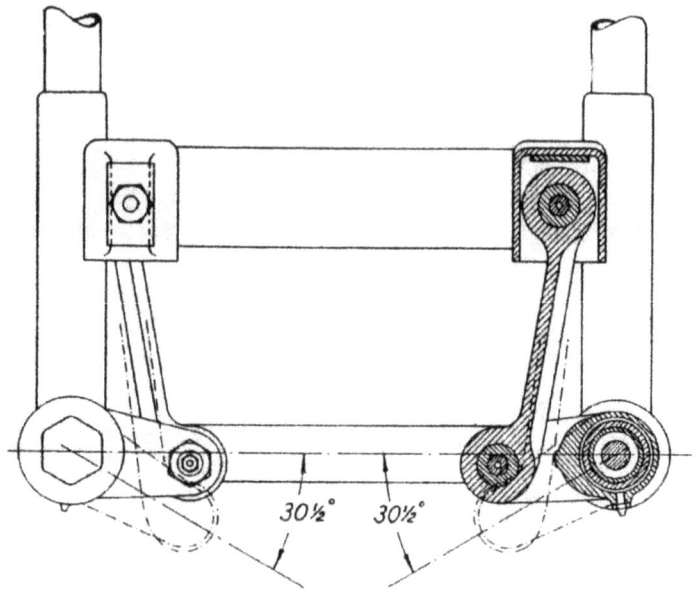

Fig. 22. REAR SUSPENSION LEVER POSITION.

horizontal as shown in Fig. 22. An easy method of checking this is to draw on cardboard a rough template with which both levers can be checked simultaneously. The forked levers can now be secured in position by the set bolts, washers and packing shims.

To cater for greater loads which may be imposed by riders over, say 14 stones, with a pillion passenger, it is permissible to increase the pre-setting by one serration, on the torsion bars. This is best achieved by following the instructions for assembly and later detaching the front anchorage lugs, having marked the positioning of the bars in the lugs. This action will revert the level of the machine to normal when fully loaded but the rate of the spring is not increased. Stronger torsion bars have been introduced on the Mark V and Plus Series machines and these have been kept interchangeable with the earlier models.

Fit the ball joints to the concentric ends of the connecting links, and place the small slotted sleeves into position, taking care to assemble these with the slots facing inwards, *i.e.* towards the ball joints. Fit the cupped washers, the larger one on the inside and the smaller on the outside, registering on the sleeves. Insert the links into position in the forks with the 'club' foot facing inwards. Fit the $\frac{7}{16}$" bolt and secure with nut and washer. The grease nipples should face towards the rear of the fork.

The rear fork can now be assembled into the frame, and the distance washer must be replaced between the fork and the frame on the right hand side. Insert the pivot pins into the frame and fork bearings with the slot in the pins registering with the locking pin holes in the frame. This applies on the early models but on the Mark IV and later models the pivot pins have annular grooves. The fit of the pin in the frame lug is such that it should require tapping home into position. Lock with the Mills pins, driving them in from the top of the lug. These pins are tapered and should therefore be inserted with the small end first. Assemble the ball joints, sleeves and cupped washers to the 'clubbed' ends of the connecting links and couple the links to the fork levers on the torsion bars.

Douglas Radiadraulic Front Fork

The Douglas Radiadraulic front fork is of the bottom link type operating coil compression springs through pistons which are oil damped to absorb the rebound. The design of the fork permits a total wheel movement of approximately 6". The swinging wheel links are coupled to the pistons through the short shaft, lever and connecting rod, as shown in Fig. 23 of this book and in plate 24 of the Spare Parts Catalogue.

REMOVAL OF FRONT FORK FROM FRAME

Support the machine by placing a block under the front end of the bottom frame members, and remove the front wheel as detailed on page 22.

Detach the head lamp by unscrewing the setscrew on either side of the headlamp mountings; the headlamp can be allowed to hang on the leads, but care must be taken to avoid damage, and this can be done by wrapping the headlamp in cloth and tying it to a suitable point on the machine where it will not be disturbed. Remove the two set bolts (24/12) which secure the bridge plate to the top of the fork legs and support the weight of the fork with any suitable object.

If the duralumin dome nut at the top of the steering column is not readily accessible due to the position of the handlebar, this should be declined to give access. To do this loosen the $2-\frac{7}{16}''$ B.S.F. nuts which secure the links to the link lugs and press the handlebar downwards. Remove the duralumin dome nut with a good fitting box spanner and this will allow the bridge plate and washer to be withdrawn from the steering column, and the speedometer to hang in a similar manner to the headlamp.

Beneath the bridge plate will be found the packing shims and adjustable cone, which should be unscrewed with the aid of a 'C' spanner or large grips, taking care not to damage the part. When the adjustable cone is unscrewed the $\frac{3}{16}''$ diameter steel balls will tend to fall away and adequate precautions should be taken to collect these. There are 24 balls on the Mark III and 22 on the subsequent models. If any are lost it is necessary to obtain a complete new set as the old must never be mixed with the new.

Remove the fork from the frame, and note that the lower inner race bearing comes away with the column. The bearings used are either of the cone and cup type with uncaged $\frac{5}{16}''$ steel balls (17 per set) or the taper roller type. These bearings are interchangeable but in the case of the cone and cup type care must be taken to collect the balls as they will fall immediately the fork is lowered.

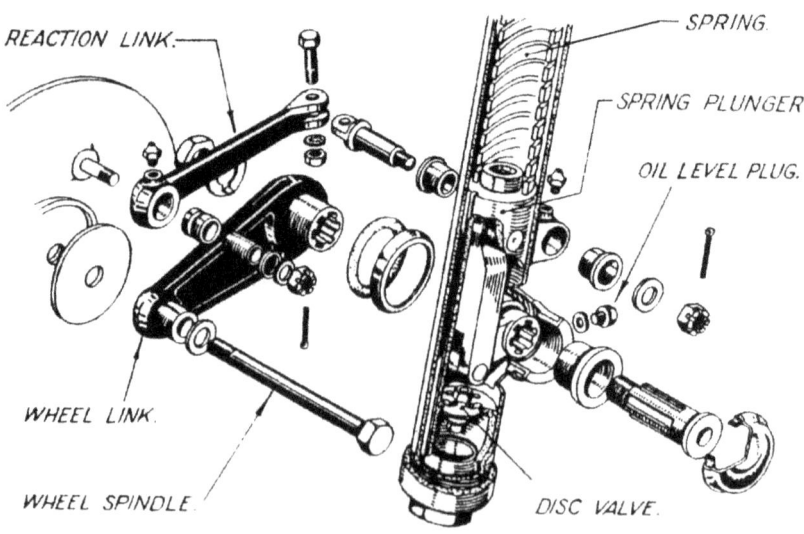

Fig. 23.   FRONT FORK. EXPLODED SECTIONAL VIEW.

DISMANTLING OF FRONT FORK

The Mark III and Mark III Sports models carry the mudguard on the fork and in these cases the mudguard should be removed from the lugs by the 2—¼" B.S.F. bolts and nuts.

Pull off the two chromed dust covers from the ends of the swinging link spindle housings, bend back the tabs of the lock washers and unscrew the two nuts which retain the links to their spindles. These nuts are found on the inside of the fork links (24/14 and 24/17). With a soft metal drift knock out the spindles and steel bushes (24/22). The bronze bushes should not be disturbed unless requiring renewal. The removal of these parts will permit the oil to drain, therefore it is advisable to place a suitable receptacle under the fork.

Remove the two end caps at the bottom of each fork leg, using a good fitting box or ring spanner. These caps have a very fine thread and therefore great care should be taken whenever removing or replacing. The plungers (24/32) and springs are now free to be withdrawn. There is an abutment plate (24/34) above each spring and if these do not come away with the springs, they should be removed to avoid subsequent loss. If necessary, remove the splined lever (24/27) from the connecting link (24/31) and the link from the plunger by drifting out the respective pins, which on the earlier models have aluminium end pads.

RE-ASSEMBLY OF FRONT FORK

The same care and attention should be given to cleaning the components of the fork as that detailed for the engine and gearbox.

For the models prior to the Mark V insert the springs into the fork members with the larger diameter to the top and registering on the spigot of the abutments situated inside the fork. The Mark V spring is parallel and selective assembly is not necessary. Fit the plunger assemblies and replace them in the fork with the non-return valve to the bottom. Tuck the levers into the plungers to enable these to be inserted in the fork. The plungers should be inserted with the levers to the rear so that they fall into the spindle housings.

Insert the steel bushes and spindles through the spindle housing and connecting rod lever; it will be necessary to apply some pressure to the bottom of the plungers to enable the splines of the spindle to marry with those of the lever. Push the swinging links on to the splines of the spindles, ensuring that the link with the pinch bolt boss is fitted to the right hand side. There should be no doubt as to the correct position of the swinging links on the splines, as these are of such a coarse pitch that an error would be obvious. Secure with the nut and lockwasher. At the other end of each spindle press on the chromed dust cover, and rubber ring, which should be moistened if any difficulty is experienced. Finally the end caps of each fork leg should be screwed home.

RE-ASSEMBLY OF FRONT FORK IN FRAME

Before inserting the fork into the frame the bearing cup in the head of the frame should be given a supply of grease and the ball bearings inserted. Give the bottom taper roller race a supply of the recommended grease or treat as for the top bearing if it is of the cup and cone type. Insert the fork and secure the assembly with the adjustable cone after ensuring that the balls are still in position. When the fork is in position it should be supported while the adjustable cone is being screwed down. The correct adjustment for the fork is that it should rotate freely and yet have no vertical or side play.

It will be necessary to ascertain the number of packing shims which are required between the cone and the underside of the bridge plate. To carry out this operation, replace the bridge plate without any shims and secure the plate by the bolts to the fork members. With the aid of a feeler gauge the space between the cone and the plate can be decided. Remove the plate, fit the correct number of shims and re-assemble, including replacing the speedometer. *Note:*—Shims are available in the following thicknesses—.0148", .028" and .064" (.376 mm., .711 mm. and 1.626 mm.).

Re-fit handlebar securely, fit headlamp, and top up the fork legs with recommended lubricant. A Douglas steering damper may be fitted to the Mark V model and is standard equipment on the Plus Series machines. The action is straightforward, it does not require lubrication, and the components may be taken off by removing the damper adjusting knob. The arrangement of the parts is clearly shown in the illustrated Spare Parts Catalogue—plate No. 38.

DISMANTLING WHEEL SPINDLES AND BEARINGS

Only in the event of ball bearing wear or other unusual circumstances should the bearing arrangements of the wheel hubs be disturbed. Great care should be taken to ensure that the various washers and distance pieces are correctly re-positioned, that the hub shells are lightly packed with the correct grade of grease, and that the bearing retaining nuts are thoroughly tightened. Reference to the illustrations in the Spares Catalogue will clearly show the general arrangement.

Front Wheel

The bearings are fitted to a hollow spindle (26/9) and separated by a distance tube (26/8), the assembly being retained within the hub by the bearing nut (26/13) which has its outer face drilled for either a peg spanner or drift. When this nut has been removed, the hollow spindle may be drifted through, allowing the two bearings, distance tube, spacing washer, felt washers and dust cap to be removed. Re-assembly is a reversal of this procedure.

Rear Wheel

The rear wheel spindle (27/8) has an increased diameter in the centre against which both bearings abut, the bearings being locked in position by a nut (27/13) at each end. Behind each nut is a spacing washer (27/12), an oil seal (27/9) and a spacer (27/10) to separate the seal from the bearing. The spindle may be removed by unscrewing either of the nuts, when it may be drifted out leaving one bearing in the hub. It will be noted that there is a distance piece inside the speedometer gearbox and another inside each oil seal. The spacing washer between the left hand bearing nut and the brake anchor plate is similar to that used behind the bearing nuts. More than one may be necessary to provide sufficient clearance between the anchor plate and the brake drum.

FAULT FINDING CHARTS

The charts on the following pages provide a logical method of diagnosing any trouble or fault which is likely to arise.

In most cases the rider will be able to remedy the fault as soon as it is discovered, but in case further information is required it will be found on the pages to which reference is made.

Where the remedy is obvious, for example, ' Sparking plug loose ' no further comment is made.

ENGINE STOPS OF OWN ACCORD

		See page
No petrol at carburettor	Petrol tank drained	75
	Petrol tap(s) accidentally closed	75
	Petrol system blocked	75
	Air holes in petrol tank cap, blocked	75
Petrol at carburettor	Air holes in top of carburettor float chamber blocked	75
	Air leak in induction system	61
	Carburettor flooding	75
	Choked main jet	25
	Spark plugs not firing	75
	Contact breaker arm sticking or points require attention	26
	Internal failure in magneto	76

Fig. 24. *Fault Finding*

ENGINE WILL NOT START

		See page
No petrol at carburettor when tickler depressed	┌ Tank empty	9
	├ Petrol tap(s) not opened	11
	└ Petrol system blocked	75
Petrol reaching carburettor — Mixture too rich	┌ Tickler used unnecessarily	11
	├ Carburettor flooding	75
	└ Air filter choked	75
— Mixture too weak	┌ Controls not set for starting	12
	├ Air leaks	61
	└ Jets blocked	25
— Spark at plugs — Spark too weak to fire under compression	┌ Dirty contact breaker points	26
	├ Leakage in high tension leads	76
	└ Electrical leakage at spark plugs	76
— Spark at plug terminals	— Defective, dirty or wet plugs	27
— No spark at plug points — No spark at plug terminals	┌ Contact breaker arm sticking or points dirty	26
	├ Magneto slip ring dirty H.T. current tracking	76
	├ Short in H.T. leads	76
	├ Short in magneto earthing switch lead	76
	└ Failure in magneto insulation	76
— Poor compression	┌ Sparking plug loose	19
	├ Valve clearance out of adjustment	19
	├ Valves sticking open	27
	├ Cylinder head—joint leaking	27
	└ Piston rings gummed in	30

Fig. 25. *Fault Finding*

ENGINE RUNS INCORRECTLY

		See page
Engine runs steadily but lacks power	Valve clearances require adjustment	19
	Ignition retarded	46
	Valves sticking open	19
	Cylinder head—joint leaking	27
	Piston rings gummed in	30
Engine hunts	Weak mixture	61
	Ignition too far advanced	46
Engine pinks or knocks	Sparking plugs sooted	75
	Ignition too far advanced	46
	Weak mixture	61
	Engine overheating, requiring decarbonising	27
Engine runs erratically — Starved carburettor	Petrol tank cap air vent blocked	75
	Obstruction in petrol system	75
Engine misfires	Faulty spark plugs	75
	Weak mixture	61
	Contact breaker points dirty or incorrect gap	26
	Occasional short in H.T. lead	76
Noises in Engine		77

Fig. 26. *Fault Finding*

Faults and Defects—Causes and Remedies

PETROL SYSTEM BLOCKED OR CHOKED

Make sure that the tank is not empty, that the taps are turned on, and that the ventilation hole in the filler cap is not blocked. Disconnect the petrol pipe at the top of the float chamber and if petrol does not flow readily close the tap and dismantle the entire system from tap to carburettor. Clear the pipes with a length of wire. Refit and check. If petrol still does not flow readily, drain off petrol, unscrew petrol tap and dismantle. Clean the tap and its filter. Strain petrol before returning to tank.

CARBURETTOR. RICH MIXTURE

Should the mixture be too rich for starting, close the petrol tap(s), open the throttle, make sure the carburettors are not choked, and rotate the engine. This will clear the cylinders. The engine may start while cleaning out the rich mixture. If it does, open the petrol tap(s) and proceed normally. Otherwise remove the plugs, clean and replace, and start again in the normal manner.

If an air cleaner is fitted, and this appears to be choked, remove filter, wash in petrol, and allow to dry thoroughly before replacing. For all other carburation faults consult the Amal leaflet supplied with the machine.

IGNITION SYSTEM

If the ignition system is thought to be the cause of difficult starting, or faulty running, close the petrol tap(s) and examine the complete system, starting at the sparking plug as follows:—

SPARKING PLUGS

Remove the sparking plugs from the cylinder heads and lay them on the engine so that the points will be visible when the engine is turned. Connect the H.T. leads. Steadily turn the engine and observe the sparking, which should occur regularly at the points. If the spark is irregular or jumps inside the plug body, dismantle, examine and clean the plugs as previously instructed in the section on 'Running Adjustments.' If there is no spark at the plug, disconnect waterproof terminal from the plug, unscrew it from the lead and hold the lead so that there is a $\frac{3}{16}"$ gap between the end of the plug lead and any metal part of the engine. Turn the engine and sparks should regularly jump across the gap. If the sparking is irregular or no sparking occurs remove the contact breaker cover and retest; if this cures the trouble the fault is in the magneto L.T. earthing switch system. Make sure that the earthing button on the handlebar is not cutting out the magneto when it is in normal or running position. The lead between the magneto and the cut-out button may require renewing, as the insulation may have perished or become damaged.

H.T. Leads

A flaw may develop in the insulation of the leads or, after prolonged service, the rubber insulation may perish, allowing the core of the high tension cable to short to earth. A very careful examination of the connections and cable should be made. Examine the contact breaker as previously advised, and the high tension pick-up brushes and slip ring. Make sure everything is clean and in correct adjustment.

If after these tests have been made, no faults have been found, and there is still no spark it is probable that the trouble is due to some internal defect of the magneto. In these circumstances it is recommended that the instrument be returned to a Lucas Depot or Dealer.

Excessive Oil Consumption

After a considerable period of operation and dependent upon the usage of the machine, the pistons, rings and barrels are likely to be worn, allowing an excessive quantity of oil to pass the pistons and become burnt in the combustion chambers. This will be evident from the blue smoke emitted from the exhaust. When new pistons and rings are fitted or cylinders have been rebored, the oil consumption will still be above normal for a period, but with careful running-in the components will become bedded together and the oil consumption will revert to normal. External losses due to leaks are easily traceable. Be certain, when rebuilding the engine that the washers at all joints are in good condition. Some of the places most likely to leak and therefore requiring particular attention when re-assembling are :—

(*a*) Crankcase joints.

(*b*) Oil pump cover joint.

(*c*) Cylinder base joints.

(*d*)) Timing cover joint.
(*e*) Gearbox footchange mechanism cover.
(*f*) The felt washer at chain sprocket end of gearbox final drive shaft.
(*g*) The oil seal at flywheel end of the crankshaft in clutch cam spigot.
(*h*) The breather (in timing cover) which, if faulty will allow crankcase pressure to build up. The disc type breather originally fitted is now obsolete but the later type gauze baffle breather has been kept interchangeable with the earlier pattern.

NOISES

After a short experience in running the machine the rider will become familiar with the normal sound, and will quickly detect any extraneous noise due to a fault. For example, a noisy engine will result if the valve clearances are not adjusted correctly, or if the adjustment on the rocker tappet screws has not been locked correctly.

If a metallic noise is heard, it is probably due to one of the following causes.

(*a*) Engine components not properly secured.
(*b*) Engine components which, through long service, have become worn and slack.
(*c*) Mechanical defect internally.

Any unusual noise should be investigated immediately and it is important that the renewal of components, or other appropriate action, is carried out without delay.

Douglas Dragonfly

MOTOR CYCLE

Maintenance Manual

DOUGLAS (SALES & SERVICE) LTD., KINGSWOOD, BRISTOL

Telephone 73013/8   Telegrams: Douglas, Kingswood, Bristol

PREFACE

This Manual, in conjunction with the Illustrated Spares Catalogue, will enable both the private Owner and the motor cycle Dealer to follow the construction and servicing. Where handed parts are mentioned these have been viewed from the saddle. As it is customary to work upon the engine from the front, great care must be exercised in identifying handed parts since the general order will, in fact, be reversed.

The most valuable axiom for the amateur mechanic is ' A little knowledge is dangerous.' The greatest enthusiasm cannot replace experience and it is strongly urged that operations are not undertaken unless there is a reasonable possibility of satisfactory completion. The DOUGLAS Specialised Dealer Scheme, augmented by the Factory's Service Department, is available for the provision of Technical information, replacement parts, and the execution of major overhauls or repairs.

September, 1955

INDEX

Section	Page
1. General description and technical data	6

2. ON THE ROAD

Filling up	7
Controls—adjustment	8
Riding	9
Running-in	10
Starting	8

3. LUBRICATION

Clutch Cam and Thrust Bearing	12
Engine	11
External points	12
Gearbox	11
Speedometer Gearbox	12
Wheels and other grease points	11

4. RUNNING ADJUSTMENTS

Brakes	17
Carburettor	20
Chain—and care of	18
Clutch Cable and Clutch	15
Cleaning machine	23
Decarbonising	21
Grinding-in valves	22
Removing carbon	21
Sparking Plugs—cleaning and type	20
Tappets	15
Valve—removal	21
Valve—refitting	22
Wheel alignment	19
Wheel hubs	17
Wheel removal—front	17
Wheel removal—rear	17
Adjustment of Steering Head	17

5. COMPLETE OVERHAUL

Clutch—removal and dismantling	28
Clutch—re-assembly and re-fitting	36
Crankcase—parting	28
Crankcase—re-assembly	31
Crankshaft—examination	30
Cylinder Heads and Cylinders—removal (*see decarbonising*)	
Cylinder Heads—dismantling	29
Cylinders—examination	30
Cylinders and Pistons—re-fitting	31
Cylinder Heads—assembly and re-fitting	32
Engine dismantling	26
Engine and Gearbox—removal from frame	25
Generator and Timing Covers—removal	26

INDEX—continued

Section	Page
5. Complete Overhaul—*continued*	
Engine—separating from gearbox	26
Engine—re-assembly	31
Engine—re-fitting to gearbox	44
Engine and Gearbox—replacing in frame	46
Final Drive—dismantling	40
Final Drive Housing—re-fitting	43
Final re-assembly of engine and gearbox	46

Gearbox

Gearchange mechanism	44
Selector mechanism	44
Dismantling	36
Shafts and Gears—removal	38
Sleeve Gear Pinion and Layshaft—re-fitting	41
Re-assembly	41

Ignition timing	34
Kickstart mechanism—re-assembly	43
Oil Pump—removal	29
Oil Pump—re-fitting	33
Pistons—removing	26
Pistons—examination	30
Pistons and Cylinders—re-fitting	31
Starting after overhaul	47
Suggestions—preparatory to overhaul	24
Timing Gears—re-assembly	32
Timing and Generator Covers—replacing	35
Wheel Spindles and bearing—dismantling and re-assembly	47
Cleaning and adjusting Distributor	34
Cleaning and re-assembling Oil Filter	36

6. FAULT FINDING

Causes and Remedies

Carburettor—rich mixture	52
Excessive oil consumption	53
H.T. Leads	53
Ignition System	52
Noises	54
Petrol System	52
Sparking Plugs	52

Charts

Engine stops of its own accord	49
Engine will not start	50
Engine runs incorrectly	51

LIST OF ILLUSTRATIONS & TABLES

Fig.		Page
1.	Lubrication Schedule	11
2.	Lubrication Diagram	14
3.	Clutch Cable Adjustment	16
4.	Wheel Alignment	19
5.	Inserting Flywheel side of Crankshaft into Crankcase	32
6.	Valve Timing Diagram	33
7.	Clutch Assembly—Sectioned View, showing Extractor and Holding Plate	37
8.	Final Drive—Exploded View	39
9.	Gearbox—Diagrammatic View	42
10.	Gearchange Mechanism	45
11.	Fault Finding Graphs	49

GENERAL DESCRIPTION

THE DOUGLAS Machine dealt with in this Manual has a 348 c.c. engine, set transversely in a duplex cradle type frame, and forming a unit with the 'in-line' gearbox.

The engine number is stamped on the top left hand side of the crankcase and the frame number is stamped on the left hand frame gusset.

TECHNICAL DATA

Cylinder Bore	2·394" (60·8 mm.)
Piston Stroke	2·362" (60·0 mm.)
Total Capacity	21·24 cub. in. (348 c.c.)
Compression Ratio	8 : 1.
Petrol Tank Capacity	5¼ gallons (23·86 litres)
Petrol Tank Reserve	¾ gallon (3·4 litres)
Engine Sump Capacity	6 pints (3·4 litres)
Gear Box Capacity	1¾ pints (1 litre) approx.
O/A Length	86" (218·4 cm.)
O/A Height	42" (106·7 cm.)
O/A Width	27" (68·6 cm.)
Wheel Base	56½" (142·6 cm.)
Ground Clearance, Max.	8" (20·32 cm.)
Ground Clearance, Min.	2¾" (7·5 cm.)
Weight Dry	365 lb. (158·757 Kg.)

Gear Ratios

1st (Low)	15·54 to 1
2nd	9·6 to 1
3rd	7·05 to 1
4th (High)	5·57 to 1

ON THE ROAD

Filling Up

A quick release filler cap is fitted to the petrol tank. To remove, rotate the cap anti-clockwise one quarter of a turn and lift off. To fill the engine sump, unscrew the oil filler plug which is situated on the front left hand side of the crankcase. Fill the sump with oil until the level reaches the upper mark on the dipstick. The lower level mark on the dipstick is the danger mark and in no circumstances should the oil level be allowed to fall below this.

For gearbox, remove domed plug by kickstart lever and fill box to overflowing. Never allow the oil level to fall below half an inch of the filler orifice.

To obtain the most satisfactory service from the machine it is essential that only lubricants of the highest quality be used as recommended on the lubrication schedule. The use of an upper cylinder lubricant is advisable during the first 1,000 miles (1,600 km.) of the machine's life and may be used regularly thereafter.

Check all the cycle parts and other items requiring lubrication as specified in the schedule.

Controls

It is advisable, before starting the machine, to spend some time sitting in the saddle to familiarise oneself with the disposition and operation of the various controls, and the ' feel ' of the machine.

An air control is fitted to the L.H. handlebar. To increase air supply, move the lever towards the rider. Also on the L.H. handlebar are the clutch lever and combined horn and dipswitch.

On the R.H. handlebar are the front brake lever and throttle twist grip control. To open the throttle, turn the top of the twist-grip towards the rider.

The footbrake pedal is placed just forward of the left footrest, and the gearchange pedal in the corresponding position on the right hand side of the machine. The kickstarter is placed a little to the rear and above the gearchange pedal and can be operated whilst straddling the machine.

Footrests, gearchange, handlebars and control levers are adjustable and should be positioned to suit the requirements of the individual rider so that he may operate each control comfortably and quickly.

These should be adjusted in the following way:

FOOTRESTS

Slacken the nut on the left footrest sufficiently to allow both footrests to turn on the serrations. Adjust as required and tighten nut.

GEARCHANGE PEDAL

Remove the neutral indicator, slacken the pinchbolt and withdraw the pedal. Refit in desired position and press well back while tightening the pinchbolt. Replace the indicator so that it registers with the button on the footchange cover when the machine is in neutral gear.

HANDLEBAR CONTROL LEVERS

Loosen the pinchscrews, set where required, and tighten the screws.

HANDLEBAR

Slacken the four bolts which clamp the bars in the lugs, adjust to required height and re-tighten.

STARTING

First ensure that the gear lever is in the neutral position. Turn on the main fuel supply by pressing the hexagon button, situated below and to the rear of the petrol tank, as far as it will go and see that the small horizontal lever above the button is turned to its full travel in an anti-clockwise direction when viewed from above.

The reserve fuel is turned on by moving this lever over to its full extent in the opposite direction.

Slightly flood the carburettor by depressing the tickler on top of the float chamber. Take care not to overflood as this will result in a rich mixture and starting will be difficult.

To start the engine under normal conditions after flooding the carburettor proceed as follows.

See that the ignition is switched on, open the air control to one third of its travel and open the throttle approximately one eighth. Smartly depress the kickstart pedal, do not kick timidly or stop before the pedal has reached the end of its travel: the engine should start after the second or third kick. After a little experience it will be found possible to set the controls to obtain a start 'first kick' result, except in the very coldest conditions.

Never ride any distance with the air lever in the closed position, as this will result in excessive petrol consumption and uneven running. Never over-rev an engine, expecially when starting from cold, always warm up gradually and thus give the oil a chance to circulate freely. To stop the engine, close the throttle and return the ignition switch to the 'Off' position, after which turn off the petrol.

Riding

To set the machine in motion, engage bottom (first) gear. To do this pull the clutch lever towards you to its fullest extent and with the right toe, lift the gear change pedal firmly upwards to the full extent of it's travel. Now let in the clutch very gently by gradually releasing the lever and, at the same time, increase the engine speed by gradually opening the throttle. This will take the machine smoothly into motion. For the best results it is necessary for all these movements to be carried out firmly and gradually.

To change into a higher gear, accelerate until the correct speed is reached (see table), then partially close the throttle and simultaneously withdraw the clutch. This will decrease the engine speed, which is necessary when changing to a higher gear. At the same time depress the gearchange pedal to the extent of its travel and retain it there while letting in the clutch. The machine will then be in second gear. Repeat this procedure for changing into third and top gears, and after every gearchange allow the pedal, which is spring loaded, to return to its free (central) position.

To change to a lower gear, withdraw the clutch, accelerate the engine, lift the gearchange pedal to the extent of its travel, and let in the clutch.

As a guide to the beginner, the following speeds are suggested as being suitable for gearchanging:

First to Second gear ..	10 m.p.h. (16 km.p.h.)
Second to Third gear ..	15 m.p.h. (24 km.p.h.)
Third to Fourth gear ..	25 m.p.h. (40 km.p.h.)

These speeds are approximate and after a time experience will dictate the speeds at which gearchanges can best be made.

To develop a neat and silent gearchange technique may take some time but this will be amply repaid by greater comfort and longer life for the machine.

Use the throttle to govern the speed of the machine: to lift the clutch and apply the brakes to slow the machine is wasteful when the same braking effect could be obtained by closing the throttle, allowing the engine to retard the machine's speed.

On greasy roads the use of the engine as a brake is to be recommended, especially for effecting a smooth change to a lower gear. To stop the engine after the machine has been brought to a standstill, engage neutral, close the throttle and switch off the engine. Turn off the petrol.

Running In

To ensure the best service and length of life from your machine, care should be taken with the running in. The engine should never be allowed to over-rev or labour, and for the first 500 miles (800 km.) it is recommended that the throttle should not be opened more than approximately half-way. The following table is given as a guide.

MAXIMUM RUNNING IN SPEEDS

	Up to 200 miles (320 km.)	200 to 400 miles (320 to 640 km.)	400 to 500 miles (640 to 800 km.)
Top gear	35 m.p.h. (55 km.p.h.)	45 m.p.h. (70 km.p.h.)	50 m.p.h. (80 km.p.h.)
3rd gear	28 m.p.h. (44 km.p.h.)	36 m.p.h. (57 km.p.h.)	40 m.p.h. (64 km.p.h.)
2nd gear	20 m.p.h. (32 km.p.h.)	26 m.p.h. (42 km.p.h.)	30 m.p.h. (48 km.p.h.)
1st (Low)	14 m.p.h. (22 km.p.h.)	18 m.p.h. (29 km.p.h.)	20 m.p.h. (32 km.p.h.)

After 500 miles (800 km.) have been covered, short bursts of speed are desirable to hasten the final bedding-down of the pistons. Gradually increase the duration of the speed bursts until the machine will stand large throttle openings for indefinite periods. Running, say, 1,000 miles (1,600 km.) at 30 m.p.h. (48 km.p.h.) will not bed down the pistons to enable them to stand continuous high speed running. Piston temperatures are the important factor and this depends not only on speed and throttle opening but also on how long that particular throttle opening has been reasonably sustained.

If the engine shows the slightest sign of slowing, ' pinking,' overheating or seizing, immediately lift the clutch and close the throttle. Serious damage may result to the pistons if the inertia of the machine forces them up and down the cylinders when they are over-expanded.

We recommend that, after the first 500 miles (800 km.) the machine be returned to the dealer who will carry out a check in accordance with the Douglas Free Service Scheme.

LUBRICATION

Engine Lubrication System

The vane type oil pump driven by a vertical shaft through worm gearing from the right hand camshaft, is situated in the sump and is completely submerged. The pump draws oil through a removable gauze filter and forces it under pressure, through internal passages to a felt sack filter, then to the front end of the crankshaft, and thence by oil ways in the crankshaft to the front main bearing and both big-end roller bearings.

The remainder of the moving parts, including the gudgeon pins, are lubricated by splash and oil mist, the surplus oil draining back to the sump. The normal oil pressure is approximately 6–9 lbs. per square inch (·42–·63 kgm./sq.cm.). The sump should be drained and refilled after the first 500 miles (800 km.) and thereafter every 2,000 miles (3,200 km.). The sump and oil ways may be cleaned by use of one of the various flushing oils: circulate the flushing oil freely by starting the engine, but do not run the engine for more than approximately one minute. Drain and refill with fresh lubricating oil as recommended. Providing these simple instructions are carried out, the rider should never experience trouble from the lubrication system.

Gearbox

After the gearbox has been filled with the recommended oil to the required level, it is only necessary to keep up the level, and drain and refill at the specified intervals. To drain, unscrew the plug situated in the right hand side of the gearbox, taking care not to lose the fibre washer on the plug. The recommended grades of lubricant are shown in the schedule.

Wheel and Other Grease Points

One stroke of the grease gun should be applied to each hub and the front and rear brake cam spindles every 2,000–3,000 miles (3,200–4,800 km.). Care should be taken not to use too much, excessive grease will work its way into the brakes, impairing their efficiency. The grease gun should also be applied to the following points, in accordance with the lubrication schedule:

Clutch Cam and Thrust Bearing

Remove the inspection cover situated on the left hand side of the clutch housing for access to the clutch cam plate bearing grease nipple.

Speedometer Gearbox

Situated on the right hand side of the rear wheel.

External Points

Use engine oil in an oil can, every 2,000 miles (3,200 km.) on the following: handlebar control levers, control cables, front brake anchorage plate (through the small grub-screw hole in the upper side of the central boss), rear brake pedal, pillion footrests.

	Summer	Winter
ENGINE Inspect level in sump every 200 miles (320 km.). Drain and refill at first 500 miles (800 km.) and thereafter 2,000 miles (3,200 km.)	Mobiloil D SAE 50 Castrol XXL SAE 40 Energol SAE 40 Essolube SAE 50 Shell X-100 SAE 50	Mobiloil A SAE 30 Castrol XL SAE 30 Energol SAE 30 Esolube SAE 30 Shell X-100 SAE 40
GEARBOX Inspect level every 1,000 miles (1,600 km.). Drain and refill every 10,000 miles (16,000 km.).	Mobiloil — Mobilube G.X. 140 Castrol — Hi-Press Gear Oil SAE. 140 Energol — B.P. Energol 140 E.P. Shell — Shell Spirax 140 E.P. Esso. — EXPEE Compound 140	

Grease Gun. Mobilgrease No. 2. Castrolease CL. Energrease C3. Esso Grease. Shell Retinax A.

Every 1,000 miles (1,600 km.). Steering Column (1). Front Brake Link (2).

Every 2,000 miles (3,200 km.). Wheel Hubs (2). Brake Cam Spindles (2). Speedometer Gearbox (1). Clutch Cam and Thrust Bearing (1).

Oil Can. (Engine Oil.) Every 2,000 miles (3,200 km.). Control Levers and Cables, Front Brake Anchorage Plate, Rear Brake Pedal, Pillion Footrests.

Fig. 1. *Lubrication Schedule*

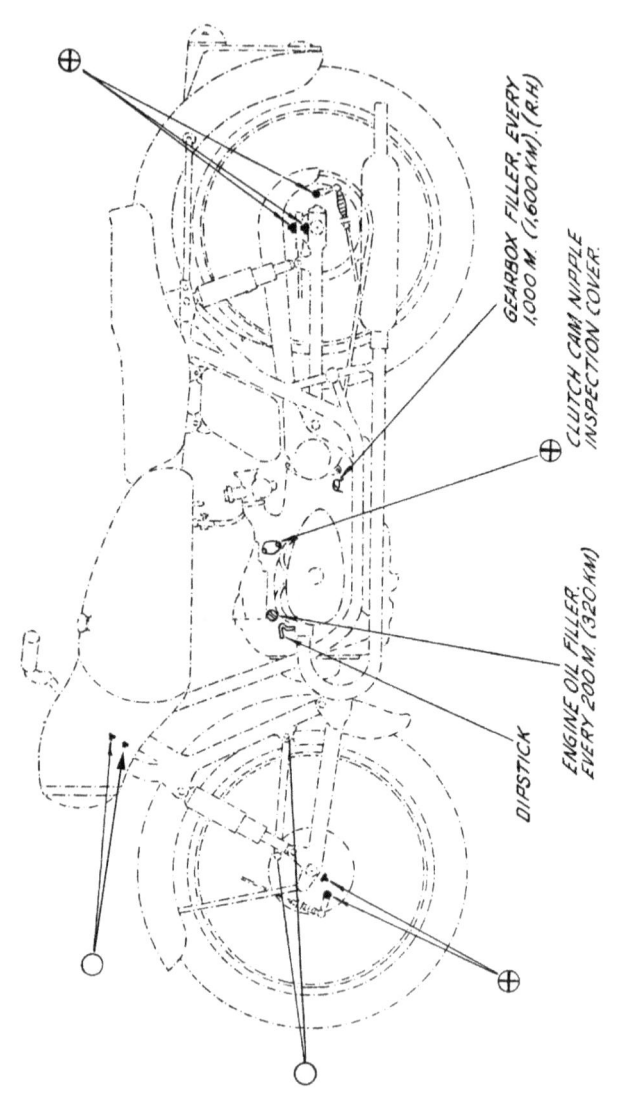

Fig. 2. LUBRICATION DIAGRAM.

RUNNING ADJUSTMENTS AND GENERAL MAINTENANCE

After the first 500 miles (800 km.) it is essential that all nuts, especially those on the cylinder heads, are checked and tightened if necessary.

Tappet Adjustment

To adjust valve clearances, remove the rocker covers by undoing the central screws with the tool provided. With the sparking plugs removed and the machine on the stand, engage top gear and revolve the engine by turning the rear wheel until the engine is at approximately top dead centre (T.D.C.) with both valves of the cylinder under observation closed (the valves of the other cylinder will be ' rocking '). The clearance between the rocker and the valve tip should be ·003" (·0762 mm.). The engine should be cold when checking tappets and a feeler gauge used. If the clearance requires adjusting, slacken the locknut on the adjustable ball and (with a screwdriver in the slot provided in the end of the ball shank) set the rocker to the gap mentioned: be sure to lock the nut securely without overstressing. Re-check the clearance, as it is possible that the tightening of the locknut may alter the clearances slightly. Similarly, check and adjust, if necessary, the clearance of the valves in the other cylinder, after making sure that the engine has been rotated one complete revolution to ensure that the valves to be adjusted are closed. Valve adjustment should not be necessary more frequently than at intervals of 2,000 miles (3,200 km.). It is essential that the joint washer be renewed if any sign of tearing is detected.

Clutch Cable Adjustment and Clutch

This is effected by the adjuster on the clutch cable which is situated on the left hand side of the crankcase bell housing. The locknut, on the adjuster, should be slackened prior to adjustment and locked after. The machine leaves the Works with the adjuster screwed out to its maximum as any wear that takes place is compensated by screwing the adjuster in or downwards.

If there is any tendency of the clutch to slip, the adjuster should be screwed inwards until there is approximately $\frac{3}{16}$" to $\frac{1}{4}$" (5–6·5 mm.) free movement of the clutch handlebar lever.

Should there be any excessive amount of backlash (free movement) of the clutch handlebar lever or if the clutch does not completely disengage, the adjuster should be screwed outwards.

A remote coarse adjustment is also provided by the swinging movement of the adjustable arm on the clutch cam. If necessary this can be reset by removing the inspection cover and slackening the $\frac{7}{16}''$ B.S.F. bolt and nut, so that the cable adjuster is screwed out fully when the wire has the correct clearance.

The clutch springs are non-adjustable as the rate of wear on the friction linings is very slight. Any wear that does occur is automatically compensated by the clutch springs, and provided the cable is maintained in correct adjustment to keep the necessary clearance for the thrust race bearing, no further adjustment is necessary until relining (see ' Overhaul ').

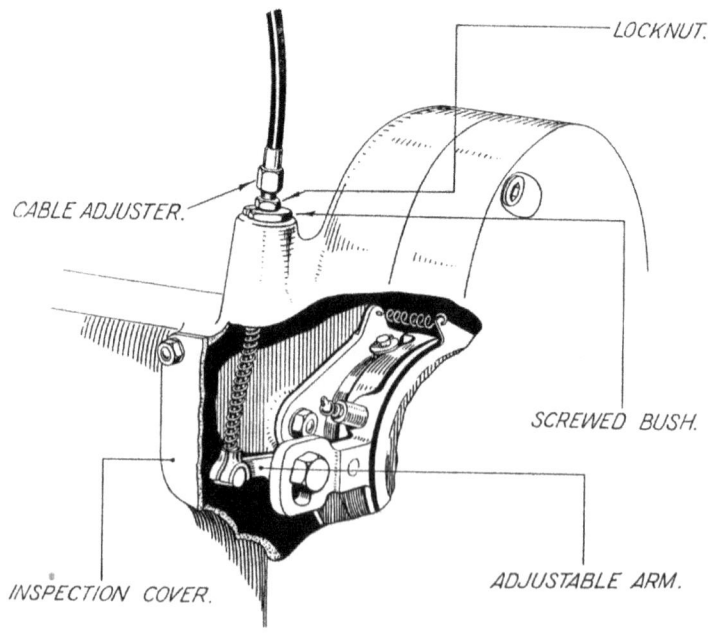

Fig.3. CLUTCH CABLE ADJUSTMENT.

Brakes

Before attempting to adjust the brakes ensure that the wheels are off the ground. When adjusting the brakes, avoid an undue amount of slack in the rear brake pedal and the front brake handlebar lever, but make sure the brakes are not binding and that the wheels are perfectly free.

Rear Brake Adjustment

An adjuster and locknut, at the rear end of the cable, controls the rear brake adjustment. Pedal stop is provided but brake cable adjustment does not vary the positioning of the pedal.

Front Brake Adjustment

The front brake is adjusted in the same way, by adjuster and locknut, at the wheel end of the cable.

Wheel Hubs

The wheel hubs are fitted with non-adjustable ball bearings and should require no adjustment after the machine has left the Works.

Adjustment of Steering Head

Remove the centre nut with washer between the handlebar lugs and lift the cover plate up to its full extent. Slacken the pinch bolt and take up any slack by tightening the serrated nut.

Care must be taken to see that the head is not overtightened so that steering is stiff.

After completion of adjustment retighten the pinch bolt. Replace the cover plate to its correct position and refit the centre bolt.

Removal of Front Wheel

It is seldom that either wheel need be removed but should this become necessary, first detach the front brake cable from the handlebar lever. Remove the bolt at the fork end of the brake torque link, and the wheel spindle nut. Remove the wheel spindle and take out the wheel. If necessary, the brake anchorage plate together with the shoes, can now be lifted from the wheel.

Re-assembly is a reversal of the above procedure.

Removal of Rear Wheel

Remove the chainguard which is secured at both ends. Disconnect the speedometer cable from the gearbox on the rear wheel and remove the chain connecting link, taking care not to lose the components. To release the brake cable from the pedal, unscrew the $\frac{1}{2}''$ B.S.F. locknut on brake pedal adjuster and slide onto cable. Ensure slot in adjuster is coincident with slot in frame lug, then depress pedal and allow it to return by pulling cable taut, this will enable ferrule to clear adjuster and cable can then be removed. Remove bottom damper bolts and the $\frac{1}{2}''$ B.S.F. bolt and flat washer which fixes the anchorage plate to rear fork, and slacken the wheel nuts. The chain adjuster nuts should not be disturbed as the chain adjuster complete will come away with the wheel, which can now be moved clear of the fork. Depress fork legs to clear anchorage plate. Wheel may then be moved clear of machine.

Refitting the Rear Wheel

This generally is a reversal of the above procedure, and should be conducted thus:—

Depress fork legs and roll in wheel, replace bottom damper bolts and secure. Fit wheel to fork and enter $\frac{1}{2}''$ B.S.F. bolt and flat washer into anchorage plate but do not tighten. Replace chain, and secure with connecting link, taking care that closed end of the spring clip is facing direction of chain travel. The wheel will assume its original position by simply pressing adjuster caps against fork ends since adjuster nuts have not been disturbed, but it is advisable to check the chain adjustment and wheel alignment as described later With the wheel correctly positioned tighten wheel nuts and anchor age plate bolt. Refit the speedometer cable and chainguard. Attach brake cable to pedal and pass cable wire through adjuster slot. Secure adjuster with locknut.

Chain

The chain should be allowed approximately $\frac{3}{4}''$ up and down play when measured mid-way between the front and rear sprockets. If there is any appreciable variation in its tension throughout one complete revolution of the rear wheel, the chain should be renewed. It is essential that the correct ' play ' is allowed at the tightest point of the chain and the machine should be off its stand for this check.

The wheel spindle nuts, the nut securing the chainguard to the anchor plate, and the $\frac{1}{2}''$ B.S.F. bolt fixing the anchor plate to the fork, must be slackened prior to varying the chain adjusters. It is advisable to pull up the chain adjuster nuts finally, after the wheel nuts have been secured.

The chain is not automatically lubricated as it is not advisable to oil from the outside—this would only encourage collection of abrasive road grit etc. It is advantageous to remove the chain, say, every 3,000 miles (4,800 km.), wash it in petrol, and soak in graphited oil overnight. After allowing to drain, it should be wiped with a rag prior to re-fitting. Remember that the closed end of the connecting link spring clip MUST be pointing in the direction of the chain travel.

Wheel Alignment

To check the wheel alignment, the simplest method is to use a cord or a long true straight edge, in the manner illustrated in Fig. 4. If any adjustment is necessary, slacken off the rear wheel spindle nuts, brake anchorage bolt and chainguard retaining nut and align the wheel by use of the chain adjuster, ensuring that the correct chain tension is maintained.

TYRE SIZE AND INFLATION TABLE

	Size	Pressure
FRONT	Standard 3·25"–19" (82 × 483 mm.)	18 lbs./sq. in. (1·266 atmhs.)
REAR	3·25"–19" (82 × 483 mm.)	22 lbs./sq. in. (1·5468 atmhs.)

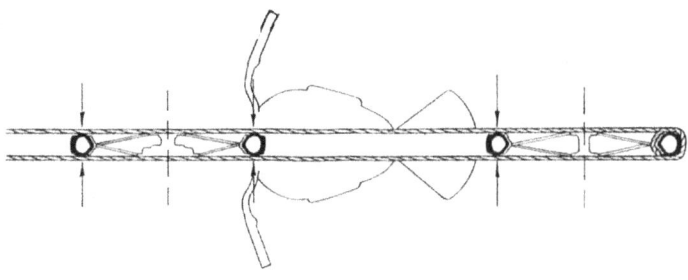

Fig. 4. WHEEL ALIGNMENT.

Carburettor

Full details of adjustment, tuning, etc., are given in the Amal leaflet supplied with the machine.

The settings are as follows:

Main Jet	130
Needle	3rd Notch
Pilot Jet	30
Pilot Outlet	·025
Needle	·1065
Throttle Valve	$3\frac{1}{2}$
Bore	$\frac{13}{16}$

Sparking Plugs. Lodge H.14S

Examine and clean the sparking plugs every 1,000 miles (1,600 km.) Disconnect the H.T. leads from the plugs by pulling off the bakelite waterproof suppressor covers, and remove the plugs from the cylinders by using a box spanner on the hexagon of the body and not on the gland nut. When dismantling the plug, it is preferable to use two box spanners; the one for the gland nut may be held in a vice.

When withdrawing the body of the electrode it is important to avoid losing the internal gas seal washer. The carbon deposit should be scraped off the inside of the body and cleaned away from the insulator, care being taken not to chip or damage the surface of the ceramic insulator. Rinse the components in clean petrol and dry off. The plug can now be re-assembled, making sure that the gas seal washer is in place.

To adjust the gap, lightly tap the points of the plug towards the central electrode until the correct gap of ·015" to ·018" (·384 to ·461 mm.) is obtained. In no circumstances should the gap be adjusted by bending the central electrode as this will result in damage to the insulator.

It is advisable to renew the sparking plugs every 10,000 miles (16,000 km.).

Decarbonising

This should be carried out approximately every 5,000 miles (8,000 km.). The following procedure should be adopted:

Disconnect the exhaust pipes, with silencers from the cylinder heads and frame. Detach the induction pipes by removing the countersunk screws from the gearbox gland and the hexagon bolts from the cylinder head gland.

Unscrew the centre screws and remove the rocker covers, paying careful attention to the joint washers to ensure these are not damaged.

Remove H.T. leads from sparking plugs and sparking plugs from cylinder heads. Turn the engine until the valves on one cylinder are closed (both valves will be then rocking on the other cylinder), Remove the rocker bearing block complete with rockers. Remove the $\frac{1}{4}''$ B.S.F. nut and washer underneath the push rod tunnel and the cylinder head and barrel base flange retaining nuts with their split washers. The head should now be free to tap off by hand (if gummed on, wait until the cylinder is removed, when the head can be tapped off the cylinder by inserting a piece of hard wood in the bore).

When the head is off, take out the push rods ensuring that they are marked to enable them to be returned to their original stations; a card marked and pierced by the push rod will suffice. Before removing the opposite cylinder head, revolve the engine until the valves are seated and then proceed as with the first head.

Remove the cylinder base nuts and washers of each cylinder. Draw the cylinders off, taking care not to let the pistons fall as they come out. The joint washers between the cylinders and the crankcase should be removed with the cylinders, otherwise the tappets may become detached from their guides, thus losing their location. Each cylinder should be marked for assembly on the correct side.

VALVE REMOVAL

It is necessary to employ a valve spring compression tool in order to clear the split valve collets. Care should be exercised in keeping the collets with the respective valves, collars and cups to ensure that they are correctly mated in re-assembly. Although the inlet and exhaust valves are interchangeable they should not become mixed.

REMOVING CARBON

Carefully scrape the carbon off the piston crowns, polish with metal polish and wash off with clean petrol. Do not use emery cloth.

Clean the carbon out of the cylinder heads and ports, using a round wire-brush and a blunt scraper. Polish the inside of the head with fine emery cloth, taking care not to touch the valve seats. Remove the carbon from the valves, taking care not to scratch or mark the seats. Polish the valve stems with fine emery, soaked in paraffin. Wash valves in petrol.

EXAMINE

Valves (stem or seat wear).
Valve guides (wear)
Fit of the pistons on the gudgeon pins.
Fit of the gudgeon pins in small end bushes.
Rings in grooves (up and down play)
Ring gaps, in cylinders (Max. gap, ·012" or ·3048 mm.). Rings should be carefully removed from the pistons for this and replaced in the same positions. New rings should have a gap of ·006" or ·1524 mm.
Pistons (conditions of skirts).
Cylinders (wear, scores).
Connecting rod play at big end bearings.

Should any of these show signs of excessive wear or play they should be renewed.

GRINDING IN VALVES

To grind in a valve, first make sure that the seat is clean, then smear a small quantity of medium grade grinding paste over the valve seat. Put the valve into its correct station in the cylinder head (taking care that the grinding paste does not reach the valve stem) and with the aid of a Suction Cup valve tool, turn the valve with a semi-rotary motion, applying gentle pressure. Lift the valve off its seat at every third or fourth reversal, frequently changing its position. When the face of the valve and the seat in the cylinder head are uniform, repeat using fine grade grinding paste.

If either the valve faces or the seats in the cylinder heads are badly pitted they should be re-faced—an operation which should be entrusted to the DOUGLAS dealer.

RE-FITTING VALVES

When all the valves are ground in, wash them and the cylinder heads to ensure that no grinding paste is left. Re-assemble as follows:

Smear the valve stem with oil and fit to its original position in the cylinder head, put on the spring assembly with the cup. The assembly comprises two springs and collar. Compress the spring with the tool, and replace the split collets.

FITTING CYLINDERS AND HEADS

The cylinder barrels can now be fitted; see that the joint washers at the base are not damaged. Examine the tappets for wear at the feet and for fit in the guides. Do not use jointing cement on the joint washers. Carefully place the cylinder on the studs projecting from the crankcase and slide the cylinder down over the piston, easing each ring in turn into the bore.

Place the cylinder head joint washer in position on the barrel over the four projecting studs. Fit the cylinder head, easing it carefully over the studs. Replace the split washers and nuts and tighten progressively. The small nut under the push rod tunnel should be left until the four main nuts are tightened.

Replace the push rods in the same order in which they were removed, ensuring that they engage with the ball head on the tappet. Place the rocker bearing block in position, again ensuring that the ball ends of the rockers are engaging in the push rod sockets. Fit shakeproof washers, nuts and finally tighten. Check valve tappet clearances and after applying a quantity of oil to the rockers, re-fit rocker covers. Finally replace cleaned sparking plugs, induction pipes and glands, making sure that the joint washers are in good condition. Re-fit the exhaust pipes and H.T. leads.

Cleaning

The appearance and value of the machine will be greatly enhanced if careful and regular attention is paid to cleaning. When enamelled or chromium plated parts are covered with dried mud, never attempt to clean the machine without first soaking the dirt with warm soapy water, then wash off with a hose or sponge and wipe the parts dry with a clean soft duster. After this the frame and chrome parts may be polished with any of the reputable polishes and chrome cleaners available. Failure to soak off carefully any mud will result in the enamel being scratched and consequent flaking off. If a hose is used, be careful to direct it away from wheel hubs and other delicate parts likely to suffer damage due to the ingress of water. Wheel spokes may be cleaned with a soft brush after soaking. To clean the engine, and any oily surfaces of the machine, wipe with paraffin, wash with water, then dry thoroughly. Occasionally paint the cylinders and heads with a good heat-resisting black, after removing any mud and oil. Air drying paint, matching the DOUGLAS colour scheme, can be used for touching up and can be obtained from DOUGLAS dealers or direct from the Factory Spares Department.

COMPLETE OVERHAUL

Suggestions

(1) A useful practice when removing any component from the machine is to temporarily replace all bolts, nuts, washers and screws to prevent loss and to label components to ensure that they are re-fitted in their correct positions.

(2) Before commencing to dismantle the machine (or any part thereof) it is advisable to remove as much dirt and mud as possible. This should be done outside the workshop, thus helping to maintain cleanliness.

(3) When carrying out a major job it will be found more convenient if the machine is placed on a firm platform approximately 15"–18" (38 cm.–46 cm.) high. This will obviate unnecessary stooping.

(4) For ease in handling the engine after removal from the frame, it is suggested that a suitable stand be made.

(5) When dismantling, all small parts should be placed in boxes allocated for each particular assembly.

(6) Where tools are necessary in addition to those supplied, the use of ring or box spanners is recommended.

(7) The following special tools are available from the DOUGLAS dealer or the Factory Spares Department.
    1. Flywheel extractor.
    2. Universal extractor for withdrawing pinions from camshaft and crankshaft.

The use of the illustrated spares catalogue in conjunction with this manual will assist in the work.

Removal of Engine—Gearbox Unit from Frame

Drain off engine oil via the drain plug provided in the rear left hand side of the sump and re-fit and tighten the drain plug, with its fibre washer. Take off the carburettor and disconnect the controls by unscrewing the capscrew, thus obviating any necessity for adjustment on re-assembly.

These control wires should be neatly coiled out of the way. Place the carburettor body aside for attention at a later stage.

Disconnect leads from battery and remove same from its carrier by unscrewing the nuts holding the top strap of the carrier, then remove battery carrier. Split battery lead running from toolbox at connector, toolbox can now be removed from machine by detaching the three fixing bolts on the top, one at the front and two at the rear. Care must be taken at all times not to scratch or damage the enamel.

Remove the clutch control cable from the handlebar lever and feed back from under tank. Disconnect leads from coil and suppressor plug caps from leads.

Remove the two round head screws from the top of the distributor cover and lift the cover up, at the same time feeding the leads through the grommets.

Remove the shock absorber cover by unscrewing the two retaining bolts and washers, then remove the chain, taking care not to lose the connecting link but to replace it on the chain. Disconnect generator leads at snap connectors under tank. The exhaust pipes should now be removed.

Before attempting to remove the footrest's spindle, which also serves as the rear mounting bolt for the gearbox, place a block of wood of suitable height beneath the gear box to take the weight of the rear end of the power unit. The left footrest can now be removed by unscrewing the nut and washer. The right footrest can now be withdrawn with the bolt, when two distance pieces and centre stand clip with backing strip, situated between the frame and the gear box, will fall away. It is essential that the distance pieces and clip are replaced in their original places as they control the positioning of the gear box in the frame.

The only attachment now holding the engine and gear box to the frame is the bolt running through the base of the crankcase sump and two brackets on the bottom frame tubes. Before proceeding further, place a support under the crankcase. Remove the nut and tap out the bolt. It will be found that there are two spacing tubes between the frame and the engine—these should be replaced on the bolt for safe keeping.

To remove the power unit from the frame it will be necessary to handle as follows. The unit is taken forward as far as possible in the frame, and the rear is lifted and brought out to the right. The lifting of the engine from the frame should not be attempted single handed.

Separating Engine from Gearbox

Before commencing to separate the engine from the gearbox, drain off the gearbox oil referred to under ' Lubrication.' These two units are held together by seven socket head screws, around the periphery of the clutch housing.

REMOVAL OF CYLINDER HEADS AND CYLINDERS (*See Decarbonising*).

REMOVING PISTONS

Remove the circlips from the pistons with the pointed nose pliers, then drift out the gudgeon pins with the aid of a soft metal punch, supporting the piston and the connecting rod on the side opposite to that at which the force is being applied. Each piston should be scratched-marked on the inside top of the skirt so that its hand can be identified for re-assembly. Each piston is stamped " front " on crown. Front being timing side.

REMOVAL OF GENERATOR AND TIMING COVERS

Remove the oil filter cap which is situated at the front of the engine below the generator cover. This cap also holds the filter in position by virtue of a coil compression spring. With the cap and spring removed draw out the filter body complete and place in a tin of petrol and leave to soak until required for re-assembly.

Take out the eleven socket screws attaching the timing cover to the crankcase and gently ease the cover away. Should the cover prove difficult, tap it sharply around the outside edge with a hide or wooden mallet. It will be found that the cover is located on the crankcase by dowels.

With the cover removed and placed on a flat surface, remove the four socket screws which hold the generator cover in position. Turn the cover over and carefully pull the generator leads through the timing cover grommet. Gently tap the generator cover off from the inside.

The generator stator is bolted to the inside of the cover and can be detached by removing the three bolts and split washers. The removal of the stator gives access to the breather which is held in position by a central screw locked by a shakeproof washer.

To remove the rotor, proceed as follows. Turn down the tabs on the locking washers under the nut on the end of the crankshaft and cam pinion bolts.

To prevent the crankshaft from rotating place a piece of $\frac{5}{16}''$ diameter copper pipe or similar ' soft ' material in the timing gears so that the crankshaft will not turn when the nut is unscrewed.

Draw the rotor off the crankshaft, taking care not to lose the key.

To withdraw the distributor idler pinion, remove the split pin from the $\frac{5}{16}''$ B.S.F. slotted nut and remove the nut, facing washer and pinion. The camshaft idler pinion is retained by a support plate which is secured by a $\frac{5}{16}''$ B.S.F. slotted nut (on the idler spindle) and two $\frac{1}{4}''$ B.S.F. nuts with shakeproof washers. Remove the nuts, the support plate, its two distance tubes and the idler pinion. With the extractor previously mentioned, withdraw the two cam pinions and remove the keys.

Pull off the crankshaft pinion and remove the locating washer and key. Tap out the taper pin in the boss of the distributor pinion and draw the pinion off the shaft.

Having done this, remove the distributor by taking out the single bolt and split washer and plain washer above the distributor body. It is important that the position of the distributor should be carefully noted so that it may be returned to its original position when re-assembling and thus ensuring that the ignition timing has been undisturbed. In conjunction with this it is advidable not to slacken the nut and bolt which hold the timing clamp and the distributor boss.

REMOVAL AND DISMANTLING OF FLYWHEEL CLUTCH

Remove the inspection cover which is situated immediately behind the right hand cylinder base; this gives access to the cable nipple which can be detached from the operating cam. Unscrew the cable adjuster bush on top of the clutch bell housing and withdraw clutch control cable.

To remove the flywheel, withdraw the split pin and remove the flywheel nut with a box spanner, holding the flywheel with the plate provided with the extractor. This plate should be secured by two $\frac{5}{16}''$ B.S.W. screws to the crankcase (see Fig. 7). Use leverage in preference to hammering but if the latter has to be adopted, several light sharp blows will be better than one or two heavy ones which might disturb the truth of the crankshaft. The flywheel and clutch assembly can now be pulled off, using the special extractor as illustrated which can be obtained from the DOUGLAS dealer or direct from the Factory Spares Department. Remove flywheel key. If it is considered necessary to dismantle the clutch, the six lock washers around the outer plate will have to be bent back and each of the six $\frac{5}{16}''$ B.S.F. nuts unscrewed progressively to release the spring pressure evenly. The pressure plate complete with the six driving studs, their bushes and shims can now be withdrawn from the flywheel, thus separating flywheel, outer plate, driven plate with friction discs and the six double clutch springs. Only if it is necessary for examination, should the operating cam and the spigot assembly be removed from the crankcase. The former is held by three small springs and the spigot assembly by three $\frac{1}{4}''$ B.S.F. nuts and split washers.

PARTING CRANKCASE

Remove the four $\frac{5}{16}''$ B.S.F. nuts and washers inside the clutch bell housing and the three $\frac{5}{16}''$ B.S.F. nuts and washers on the underside of the crankcase. With the connecting rods at T.D.C. and holding the crankcase by the timing section, allow a little clearance between the case and the work bench and gently tap the timing end of the crankshaft with a hide or rubber mallet, when the two portions should part. It is important, when carrying out this operation not to allow the crankshaft and flywheel section to fall any distance as this will cause damage. As a further precaution, place a sack or pad of cloth on the bench beneath the crankcase.

The two camshafts can now be withdrawn from their bushes. To remove the crankshaft from the flywheel section of the crankcase, ensure that the connecting rods are at T.D.C. and support the case with the clutch housing uppermost and, allowing sufficient clearance between the shaft and the bench, knock out the crankshaft with the aid of a mallet or a hammer and soft drift. Here again, it is advisable to place a sack on the bench to avoid damaging the crankshaft. The ball bearing will probably come away with the crankshaft but if it does not, it can be drifted out of the crankcase.

It is advisable upon removal of the crankshaft to tape the timing journal and timing end of crankshaft so as to prevent the entry of dirt, etc., into the oilways. Then carefully wrap the shaft in clean cloth and put it on one side.

REMOVAL OF OIL PUMP

The oil pump situated on the underside of the crankcase is retained by three $\frac{1}{4}''$ B.S.F. nuts and spring washers. Removal of these will permit the withdrawal of the cover plate and paper joint washer, leaving the oil pump body together with the cork joint washer, to be gently eased off its three studs. It is advisable at this point to replace the cover on the pump body, retaining this by three nuts and bolts, thus preventing the entry of dirt and the loss of the two vanes and their springs.

DISMANTLING THE CYLINDER HEADS AND ROCKER BEARINGS

Check the rockers for play in their bearings, as there is no necessity to dismantle these unless excessive play has developed. If it is necessary to dismantle the rocker bearing assembly remove the 2 B.A. bolts, nuts and split washers. The bearing (cap and base) can now be parted and the rockers removed, with the use of a valve spring compression tool. The valves, their springs, collars, cups and collets should be segregated in order that they may be re-assembled in their original stations.

CRANKSHAFT

Check the connecting rods for slackness or roughness on the crankpin roller bearings. If for any reason the crankshaft has to be dismantled, it will be necessary to return the assembly to the DOUGLAS dealer, who will supply a service exchange shaft. Check the connecting rods for alignment, by passing a gudgeon pin or straight bar of $\frac{5}{8}''$ (15·875 mm.) silver steel through the small ends of both rods. Check both main bearings for wear. Should the main ball bearing need renewing, it will have to be drawn off the crankshaft by an extractor tool and the new one fitted by a press to ensure that the crankshaft is not disturbed out of truth. It is important, also, to set the oil thrower so that its two small holes are not shielded by the web of the crankshaft.

PISTONS

Examine:

Fit of the pistons on the gudgeon pins.
Fit of the gudgeon pins in small end bushes.
Pistons, for condition of skirts. Rings in grooves (up and down play).
Ring gaps in cylinders. Rings should be carefully removed from the pistons for this and replaced in the same position.
Note: Max. gap, ·012″ or ·3048 mm. New rings should have a gap of ·006″ or ·1524 mm.

CYLINDERS

If possible check with the aid of a dial type cylinder gauge the cylinder bores, and if the diameter at any point throughout the length of the piston travel exceeds 2·404″ (61mm.) either new barrels will be required or the originals must be rebored and have over-sized pistons fitted.

MISCELLANEOUS

Check to ensure that all pinions are in good condition and that there is no sign of excessive wear on the teeth.

It is essential when rebuilding that every precaution be taken to ensure freedom from dirt and dust, as satisfactory operation is dependent on this. Immediately prior to rebuilding it is advisable to re-wash components, especially if there has been any lapse of time since the previous washing. During this final wash, all oil passages of the crankcase must be thoroughly syringed through. Have available a quantity of clean engine oil and give all bearings, pistons, etc., an initial coating of oil, also with the aid of a force feed oil can, squirt a quantity of oil into crankshaft oil passages.

Re-assembly

CRANKCASE

Before inserting the crankshaft into the flywheel section of the crankcase ensure that the main bearing ballrace is home on the crankshaft journal. Heat the crankcase in clean boiling water and insert the crankshaft ball bearing into its housing as far as possible. Have available a tubular distance piece and draw in the crankshaft with the aid of the crankshaft flywheel nut. Do not in any circumstances, attempt to force the crankshaft into the crankcase by hammering on the timing side end. It is important when carrying out this operation that the connecting rods are at T.D.C. and correctly positioned in relation to their cylinder spigots—the left hand cylinder is offset forward—and that the connecting rods do not become jammed against the crankcase face.

Fit the camshafts into their respective bushes in the flywheel half of the crankcase ensuring that the camshaft with the pump worm is on the left hand side. Lightly smear the joint faces with a good quality jointing cement, taking care not to allow any to enter the drilled oil ways, and carefully place on new paper joints. The timing section of the crankcase can now be fitted, making sure that the connecting rods are clear of the crankcase halves, i.e., at T.DC. and that the four drilled dowels register correctly. The crankcase assembly can now be secured by the seven $\frac{5}{16}$" B.S.F. nuts and flat washers.

PISTONS AND CYLINDERS

Refit pistons, but take care to support the connecting rods when tapping in the gudgeon pins, for which a soft metal drift should be

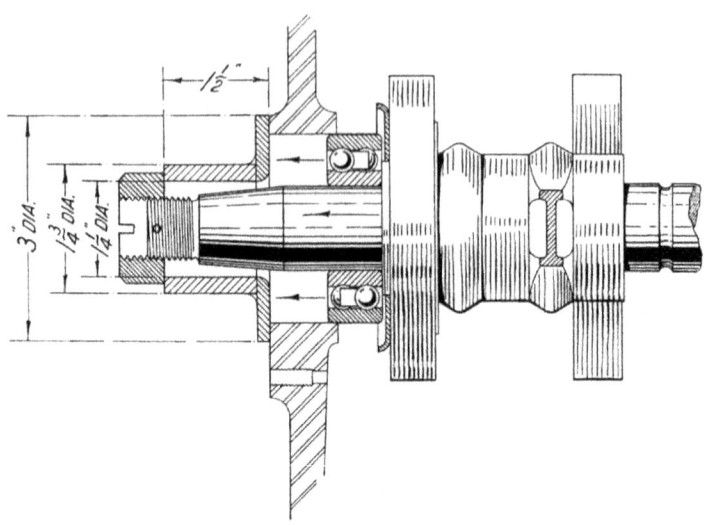

Fig. 5.   INSERTING FLYWHEEL SIDE OF CRANKSHAFT INTO CRANKCASE.

used. The pistons should be warmed, preferably in hot water, to ease the fitting of the gudgeon pins.

Fit new circlips to retain gudgeon pins, ensuring that they are correctly located in their grooves. It is essential that circlips are renewed after their original use. Place the joint washer on the cylinder and insert tappets into their housings.

CYLINDER HEADS

Having ground in the valves refit them and the springs to the cylinder heads. Refit heads to barrels and proceed as described under decarbonisation.

REPLACEMENT OF VALVE TIMING GEARS

Place the location washer over the timing end of the crankshaft and fit the key. Using a hollow drift, tap the cam drive pinion on to the end of the crankshaft and make sure that the timing mark is on the outside. Insert the parallel keys into the camshafts and fit the cam pinions by tapping on, again ensuring that the timing marks are on the outside and the pinions fitted to their respective shafts. In fitting these pinions the one with the 'line' timing mark fits on the right hand shaft (facing the engine, left hand) and the one with the 'circle' timing mark on the other shaft. Now place the camshaft idler pinion on its bush, so that it meshes with the two camshaft

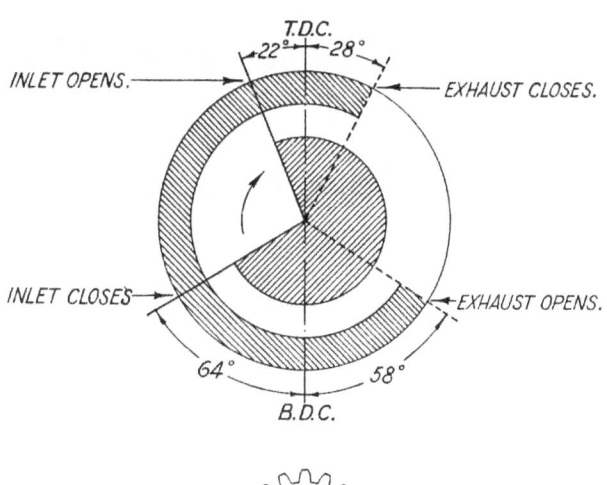

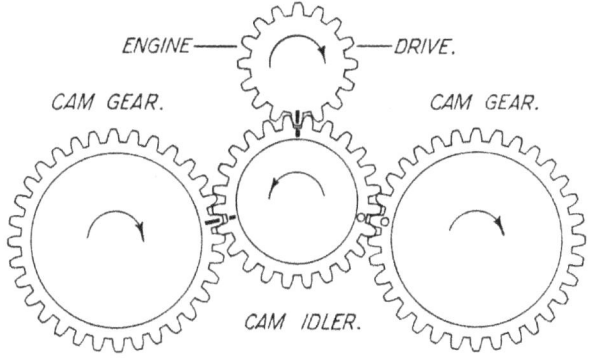

Fig. 6.   **VALVE TIMING DIAGRAM.**

pinions and the crankshaft pinion. It is important that the timing marks on the teeth of the two camshaft pinions, the camshaft idler pinion, and the crankshaft pinion, are coincident. Secure cam and idler pinions by their respective setscrews, nuts, tab washers and split pins. Do not forget to fit the two distance pieces and to secure the camshaft idler pinion strap plate by its two ¼" B.S.F. nuts and shakeproof washers.

OIL PUMP

Fit the cork joint washer so that the holes coincide with those of the pump (it is not an equilateral triangle) and then insert the oil pump, making sure that the oilways line up. Having checked that the two vanes and springs are *in situ* fit the paper washer between pump and cover plate and secure with the three ¼" B.S.F. nuts and spring washers.

TAPPET ADJUSTMENT

Set tappet clearances as previously instructed.

CLEANING AND ADJUSTING DISTRIBUTOR

Clean the outside of the distributor and wipe dry. Remove the cap by sliding off the wire retaining clip. Clean the inside of the cap with a non-fluffy petrol soaked rag and scrape the contacts inside the cap lightly to remove scale. Examine H.T. leads and renew if there is the slightest sign of cracking or deterioration.

Take off the distributor rotor arm and clean off the scale, taking care not to damage the contact spring.

Hold the distributor in a vice, using wood or aluminium in between the vice jaws and the spigot of the distributor to prevent damage.

Remove the breaker points, clean and reface with a carborundum stone. Clean out the inside of the body with petrol and dry off. Oil the spindle and the advance and retard mechanism and apply a few drops of oil to the cam lubricating pad.

Refit the points and adjust the gap to ·015"·018" (·384/·461 mm.).

IGNITION TIMING

The next stage is ignition timing which is carried out as follows.

The ignition timing, which is fully automatic, is not marked. The degree of advance is governed by the engine R.P.M. When replacing distributor see that the oil sealing ring is seating correctly in its groove. Carefully feed the distributor spigot into its housing and secure by replacing the bolt, plain washer and spring washer and provisionally tighten with the clamp in a central position. Place the distributor gear in position and fit the taper pin. When driving the pins in support the opposite side of the gear boss to take the shock and so prevent bending of the shaft. A degree plate must be used for timing and this can be attached to either the timing or flywheel end of the crankshaft. The accuracy necessary to achieve the correct distributor timing cannot be overstressed and, for this reason, piston movement down the cylinder cannot be relied upon as means of measurement as any small build up of wear at many points could total several degrees.

The engine should now be rotated until the L.H. piston is at

T.D.C. on the firing stroke (with valves rocking on R.H. cylinder).

Careful note should now be made of the relationship between the degree plate and the crankcase. Rotate the crankshaft almost two revolutions and stop it at 5° before T.D.C. Rotate the distributor gear in a clockwise direction until the contact breaker points are just opening when the rotor arm is pointing to the L.H. cylinder. Slip the idler gear into position and fit the facing washer and slotted nut, but do not split pin at this stage.

Slacken the bolt holding the distributor clamping plate to crankcase, this will permit the distributor to be moved either to the left or right for final correct timing, i.e., points just opening 5° before T.D.C. After completion of timing tighten the slotted nut and replace the split pin. Refit the cap on the distributor and slide the wire retaining clip into position.

Replacing the Timing and Generator Covers

After cleaning timing and generator covers and all relevant items, refit the breather with its round head screw and shakeproof washer. Place the stator in position with the leads uppermost and fit the split washers and bolts. Fit the generator cover, complete with stator and breather, into the timing cover using a new paper joint and a smear of good quality jointing cement, and secure with the four Allen socket screws.

Place the distance piece and rotor key in position on the crankshaft. Slide the rotor onto the shaft, fit a new tab washer and screw on the nut. Finally tighten and lock by turning up the tab.

Before placing the covers in position see that the lead from the generator stator is threaded through the grommet in the timing cover. Fit a new paper joint using jointing cement as before and place the cover on the dowels in the crankcase. Fit the eleven Allen socket screws and finally tighten progressively.

Cleaning and Reassembling Oil Filter

Remove the locking wire from the wing-nut and the wing-nut from the centre spindle. Take off the fibre washer and the end cap and remove the felt washer behind it. Draw off the filter gauze and element, the bottom cap is part of the centre spindle assembly, but the felt washer in the bottom cap must be taken out and cleaned together with the rest of the parts. The filter element inside the gauze barrel is easily removed.

After thoroughly cleaning all parts and rinsing in petrol, assemble as follows.

See that the neoprene seal is intact and fit it to the end of the filter below the bottom cap. Place the felt washer in the cap, slide the element into the gauze barrel and place these on the spindle. Fit the felt washer to the top cap and place the cap on the spindle, then the fibre washer and lastly the wing-nut. See that all parts are in alignment and tighten the wing-nut but be careful not to overtighten. Finally, secure the wing-nut with locking wire.

Insert the filter into the crankcase with the wing-nut facing outwards. Place the spring on the end of the filter and insert the cap with the fibre sealing washer, screw up and finally tighten.

Flywheel Clutch

If the clutch operating cam spigot has been removed, replace with the three $\frac{1}{4}''$ B.S.F. nuts and spring washers. Insert the operating cam assembly and attach by the three springs. Fit the control cable into the clutch housing, coupling the nipple to the operating arm. To assemble the clutch, lay the pressure plate on the bench with the six driving pins uppermost and place on the driven plate with its splined boss downwards. Fit the flywheel over the driving pins, making sure that the line mark on the periphery is coincident with that on the pressure plate. Place the twelve (six pairs) springs in the housings in the flywheel and the six shim washers on the driving pins, again ensuring that the index mark registers with those on the other two components.

With the aid of a suitable clamp (this can be made from two strips of steel, a long bolt and nut), the assembly can be compressed and the six nuts and lockwashers fitted.

Fit the woodruff key in the crankshaft, ensuring that there is no side play. If for any reason a new key is used, care must be taken to see that there is a slight clearance between the top of the key and the flywheel key-way. The whole clutch assembly should now be fitted to the crankshaft. ' Scotch ' the flywheel as previously described and tighten up the flywheel nut, using leverage rather than the hammer.

Lock with the split pin.

Dismantling the Gearbox

Withdraw the cotter pin, which is secured by a nut and washer. Remove the kickstart lever and spring. Remove the footchange

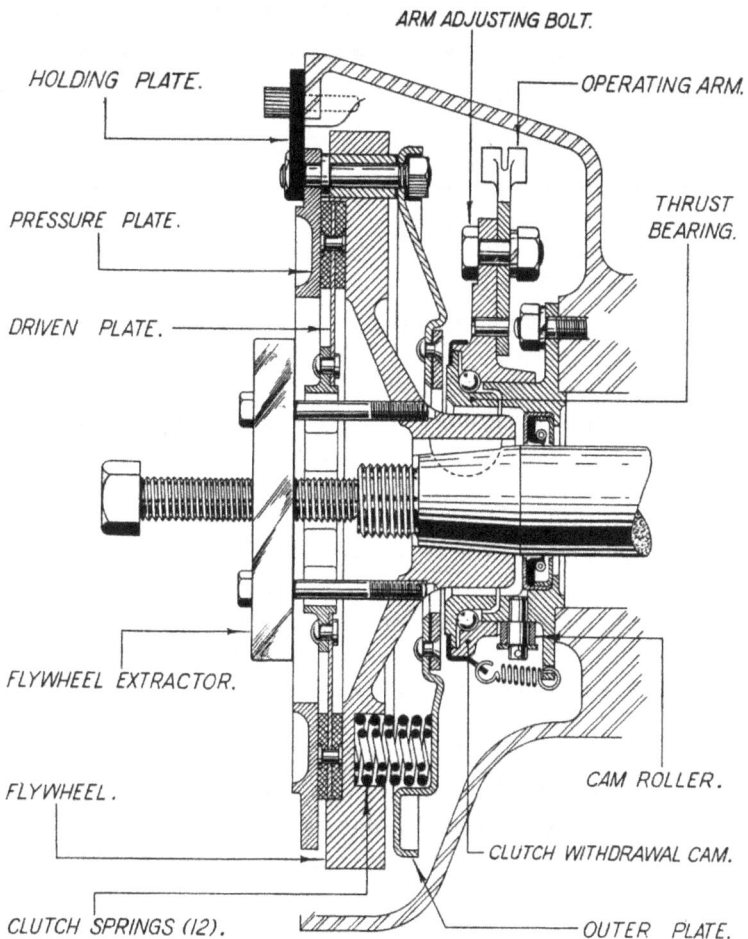

Fig. 7. CLUTCH ASSEMBLY SHOWING EXTRACTOR AND HOLDING PLATE.

pedal and cover, taking out the six socket-headed screws, when it will be possible to proceed with dismantling the remainder of the selector mechanism.

Remove the selector spindle retaining plug situated in the gearbox coverplate in the bell housing, and withdraw the spindle using a $\frac{5}{16}''$ B.S.F. bolt and a piece of tube as a drawbolt—the end of the spindle is drilled and tapped. Remove the selector forks, lifting the front one to clear the spring and plunger, which should also be removed. To remove the shock-absorber unit: lock the gear train by sliding the pinions to engage two gears simultaneously. Remove the split pin and nut, leaving the shock-absorber components free to be withdrawn from the splined sleeve on the final drive spindle: the sleeve will remain attached to the spindle. With the peg spanner provided, unscrew the duralumin plug at the other side of the gearbox and, using a drift of soft material, tap the final drive spindle through from the sprocket end and withdraw it from the opening made by removing the duralumin cap. It will be seen that as the spindle is being tapped out, the splined sleeve is left behind, and when the spindle has passed completely through, this sleeve is free to be lifted from its engagement with the hollow shaft to which it is tongued.

Unscrew the six $\frac{1}{4}''$ B.S.F. nuts and remove the final drive bevel gear and housing complete, taking care not to damage the brass shims and joint faces of the housing and gearbox case.

Take out the three Countersunk screws in the end cap at the rear of the gearbox behind the kickstart spindle. Withdraw the cap, thus exposing the kickstart auxiliary shaft, in the end of which is a small horizontal locating pin. Draw the auxiliary shaft out, releasing the kickstart bevel pinion, the kickstart gear and the thrust washer.

Remove the nut and washer from the kickstart shaft. Using a soft drift and light hammer, tap the end of the shaft and drive it out of the kickstart bevel gear and withdraw the kickstart shaft from its bush. Do not lose the key in the tapered end of the shaft. Turn down the tabs on the ends of the main and layshafts locking washers and remove the nuts, the gears being first locked as previously described. The layshaft kickstart gear, bush, spring and ratchet can now be removed but the gear on the mainshaft requires special attention: this is dealt with later.

If it is considered necessary to examine the main shaft roller bearing, the splined coupling should be removed at this stage, as it is a difficult operation when the train of gears is out of the box. To remove the splined coupling, lock the gear train and remove the large hexagon nut, using a good fitting box spanner. With the aid of an extractor the coupling can now be removed. Care should be exercised to prevent damage to the oil spinner mounted upon the coupling.

Note.—The centre bolt of the extractor should not bear directly on the end of the sleeve pinion but a suitable distance piece should be employed.

Unscrew the six $\frac{1}{4}''$ B.S.F. nuts and split washers holding the cover at the front end of the case; the layshaft, mainshaft and gears are now ready to be withdrawn.

Support the bell housing of the gearbox on two stout pieces of wood, allowing clearance for the subsequent withdrawal of the gearbox end cover. To remove the gearbox end cover together with the gear train it is necessary to tap the end of the mainshaft (which has had its nut refitted to prevent bruising of the thread) using a hammer and drift. A few sharp blows should be sufficient to release the assembly, comprising shafts, gears and cover, leaving behind the mainshaft bevel gear which is a press fit in the bearing. The bevel gear may be released by several light taps on a long drift inserted from the front of the case. The box is now completely dismantled with the exception of the sub-assemblies and the bearing retaining plate.

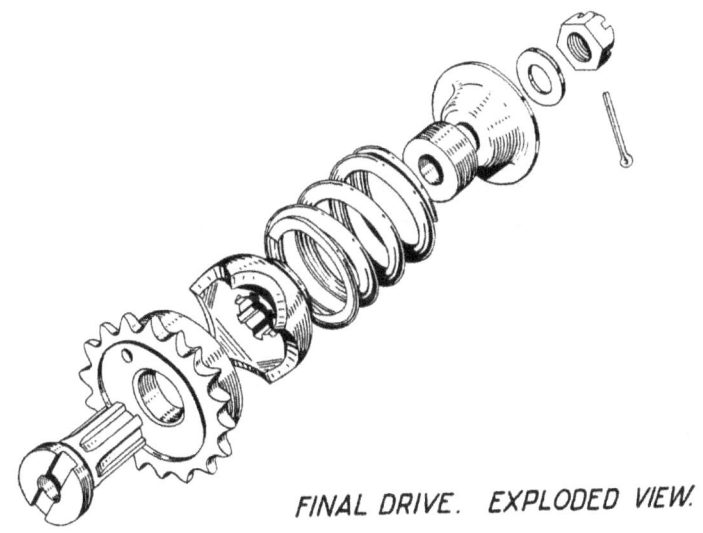

FINAL DRIVE. EXPLODED VIEW.

Fig. 8.

To complete the dismantling of the mainshaft, withdraw this with its bush from the sleeve pinion. The two sliding gears can then be drawn off their splines. The large gear together with spacing washer at the final drive end can also be withdrawn. The bronze bush and the inner thrust washer remain on the mainshaft and can be removed by an extractor, placed over the thrust washer.

To dismantle the layshaft, first revolve the sleeve pinion until the flat machined in the oil thrower is linable with the layshaft ball bearing. The layshaft with its ball bearing may now be withdrawn from the end cover, after which the two end gears may be drawn off and the two sliding gears removed.

If the splined coupling has been removed as previously described, access to the sleeve pinion roller bearing can now be obtained by removing the countersunk headed screws securing the bearing retaining plate. The shaft complete with spinner, bearing rollers and felt oil seal, should now be drawn out of the gearbox end cover.

To replace either the main or layshaft rear bearings it is necessary to remove the bearing retaining plate by unscrewing the countersunk screws.

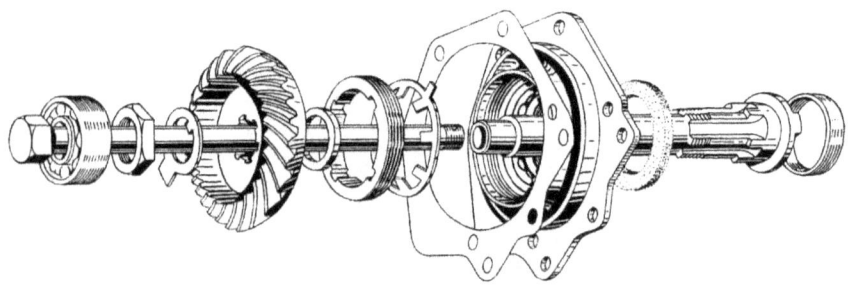

Final Drive

To dismantle the final drive unit (when this is removed from the gearbox) bend back the tabs of the lock washer and unscrew the nut securing the bevel gear to the hollow shaft. To do this, replace the splined sleeve and final drive bolt, using a distance piece to compensate for the components not included. Hold the splined sleeve in a vice with soft jaws (or use copper clamps). With the nut removed draw the bevel gear off its splines, and remove the distance piece situated between the ball race and bevel gear, after which the shaft is free to be pushed out of the bearing. If it is necessary to extract the ball bearing, unscrew the large ring nut which becomes visible after removing the bevel gear. The bearing can now be taken out.

If at any time the felt oil seal ring needs renewing, it will be necessary to dismantle the final drive unit as far as the removal of the hollow shaft. Care must be taken to avoid cutting the felt washer when the sleeve is re-assembled.

Re-assembly of Gearbox

Treat the dismantled components in a similar manner to those of the engine unit, i.e., wash off thoroughly, and examine for any signs of wear. Renew where necessary.

When re-assembling give all components an initial supply of oil. If new bearings have been fitted to the rear end of the gearbox, replace the bearing retaining plate and secure with countersunk screws, caulking the plate into the screw slots.

To re-assemble the final drive unit, insert the bearing in its housing, and secure with the large ring nut and lock washer. Insert the hollow spindle and press home into the bearing with the dogs facing outwards and with the oil seal sleeve tube in position. Place the distance piece over the shaft, and press the bevel gear onto the splines, securing it with the hexagon nut and tab washer.

To assemble the layshaft, place on the sliding gears, ensuring that the larger diameter gear is to the front portion of the shaft. Insert the two woodruff keys at either end of the shaft and press on the gears with the boss of each outermost. Fit the distance washer and press home the front ball bearing.

RE-ASSEMBLY OF SLEEVE GEAR PINION AND LAYSHAFT INTO COVER

Ensure that the oil seal is in position. Place the spinner on the shaft with the lip facing forward and fit the bearing retaining plate. Apply a liberal quantity of good quality vaseline to the roller track, then around the track of the shaft place the eighteen $\frac{1}{4}''$ diameter rollers. Push home the shaft, complete with rollers, spinner and retaining plate. A useful method for entering the bearing rollers into their outer track is to fit an elastic band around the row of rollers, cutting this band to facilitate its removal when the rollers have entered. The layshaft assembly should now be fitted to the cover. Thread the sliding gears on to the mainshaft, with their dogs outermost, and the larger gear to the rear. Insert the front end of the mainshaft, with its bronze bush, into the sleeve gear pinion.

Fit on the large low gear pinion, at the rear of the shaft, with its

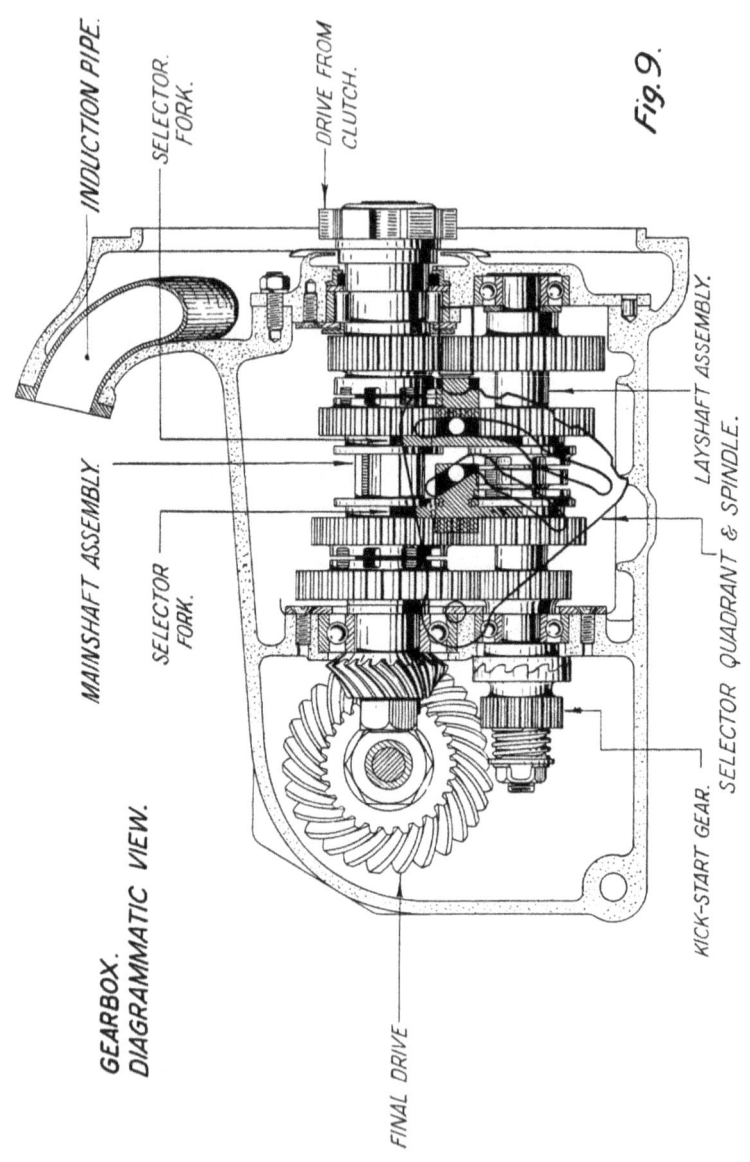

Fig. 9. GEARBOX. DIAGRAMMATIC VIEW.

dogs facing inwards. Fit the outside thrust washer with its oil slots against the gear.

Fit the mainshaft bevel to its bearing. To do this it may be necessary to use the draw bolt, which is simply a long threaded bolt, with a suitable large washer at either end, and nut.

Replace the front cover assembly, comprising the mainshaft and layshaft units, taking care that the joint washer has been fitted to the cover and that the two shafts enter their respective locations. It may be necessary to drift the mainshaft home into its bevel gear. Secure the cover with the six $\frac{1}{4}''$ B.S.F. nuts and spring washers. Insert the key into the driving shaft and fit on the splined coupling, securing it with the large hexagon nut. This nut should be tightened with the aid of a box spanner, whilst the gears are locked in the manner already described. With the shaft still locked press on the layshaft kickstart ratchet. Place the kickstart ratchet pinion spring onto the pinion bush followed by the ratchet pinion itself and place this assembly on the layshaft. Fit a new tab washer, screw on the nut, finally tighten and turn up locking tab.

RE-ASSEMBLY OF KICKSTART MECHANISM

If there has been any sign of an oil leak on the kickstart shaft, renew the felt seal in the bush. Insert the kickstart shaft into the bush, place the key in the taper and fit the bevel gear, tab washer and nut and finally tighten.

Turn up the locking tab. Refit the kickstart lever and returning spring and replace cotter with nut and washer.

Take the kickstart auxiliary shaft, after smearing with oil, thread on the bevel pinion, the kickstart gear, the thrust washer and insert the end of the shaft in its location in the gearbox. It is important that the kickstart pedal should be in the ' up ' position and that the gap in the teeth of the kickstart pinion should be placed so that the ratchet pinion on the layshaft is free to rotate.

When this is done, replace the end cap at the same time ensuring that the pin in the end of the auxiliary shaft enters its locating slot in the cap. Replace the countersunk screws and finally tighten.

HOUSING ASSEMBLY

Fit the final drive bevel and housing assembly into position in the box, replacing the same number of shims as found when dismantling. When driving the hollow shaft into the ball bearing on the kickstart side of the box, care must be taken to ensure that the shaft enters the ball bearing squarely, and that the teeth of the bevels are in mesh. Secure the assembly in position and insert the final drive spindle from the kickstart side, if necessary gently tapping home until the hexagon head rests against the bearing. Tighten all nuts. Press on the splined shaft at the shock-absorber end of spindle so that the slot mates with the dogs in the hollow spindle; if necessary tap home gently before placing on the sprocket with its cam lobes facing outwards. Push the shock-absorber cam on to the splines so that the lobes mate with the sprocket. The assembly of this section should be completed by placing on the distance piece, spring and end cap, securing these with the $\frac{1}{2}''$ B.S.F. nut, washer and split pin.

RE-ASSEMBLING SELECTOR MECHANISM

The plunger, spring, selector forks and supporting spindle can now be fitted. Note that the driving pins of the forks are fitted facing each other and the actual forks locate in the annular grooves of the sliding pinions. The forks can be identified by the fact that the front fork (third and top gears) has its driving pin nearly in line with the fork but in the case of the rear fork (first and second gears) the driving pin is well off centre. Tap home the selector spindle and finally locate it by screwing tight the aluminium plug. To lock the plug, it is advisable to lightly caulk the metal of the cover plate to the screwdriver slot of the plug.

The aluminium cap at the kickstarter end of the final drive spindle can now be replaced and secured with the aid of the peg spanner.

Rejoining the Engine and Gearbox

Before proceeding any farther with the assembly of the gearbox it is necessary to bolt the engine and gearbox units together.

With the engine resting on the bench centralise the clutch plate by disengaging the clutch (through the clutch inspection housing).

Join the gearbox to the engine unit so that the splined coupling on the gearbox sleeve pinion mates up with the splined boss of the clutch plate. Press home the gearbox into the spigot of the bell housing and insert the socket head screws. Tighten these gradually, working around until they are all quite tight.

GEARCHANGE MECHANISM

The gearchange mechanism should now be added, but before so doing it is necessary to remove the selector quadrant from the assembly, as this must be located separately. To do this, remove the neutral indicator and carefully pull off the selector quadrant, which is secured by a parallel key and should withdraw fairly easily. The selector quadrant should now be fitted to the gearbox and the gear selected for this should be neutral. There are several indentations in the edge of the quadrant and neutral gear is the second indentation from the bottom. Engage the quadrant spindle into its bush in the gearbox but before pressing it right home it is necessary to lift the gear location plunger which is spring loaded. This can be done by levering with a screwdriver. The quadrant can now be fully engaged, but it is necessary to ensure that the selector fork driving pins engage with the cam tracks in the quadrant. Fit the gear change cover, making sure that the spring on the outside spindle of the quadrant does not become detached and that the joint washer is in correct position. Secure the cover with the six socket head screws. Fit the gearchange pedal with its felt washer, and the kickstart lever.

Fit both induction pipes in the manner already described under decarbonisation.

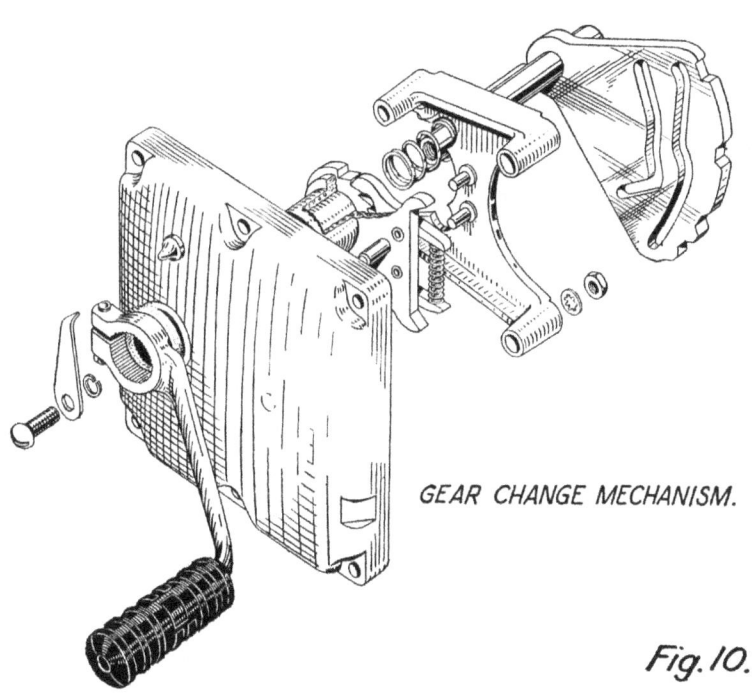

GEAR CHANGE MECHANISM.

Fig. 10.

Replacement of Engine-Gearbox Unit in Frame

The complete unit is now ready for replacement in the frame, and this should be done in the following manner: Working from the right hand side of the machine insert the unit diagonally, locating the timing cover between the frame down tubes. Now lift the rear portion of the gearbox so that it will clear the pivot point of the rear suspension, and when it is within the confines of the frame, lower the gearbox into position. Before installing the power unit a block of suitable height should be placed between the bottom frame members to take the weight of the engine and gearbox until the mounting bolts have been fitted. The front mounting bolt, with its two spacing washers, should be fitted first and the nut and washer screwed on, but not finally secured. The rear mounting bolt, which also has the right side footrest attached, should then be inserted, ensuring that the distance pieces are fitted in correct sequence at both sides of the gearbox with the spring clip and backing strip located between frame and R.H. distance piece, backing strip outwards. Fit left side footrest and after adjusting for position, secure the assembly with the nut.

Final Re-assembly

Replace toolbox, battery carrier and battery, but as a safety precaution, do not connect battery leads until machine is ready for final check over.

Pass clutch control wire through aperture in distributor cover and refit wire to handlebar lever. Adjust clutch if necessary as described under Running adjustments.

Pass ignition leads through grommets in distributor cover prior to finally replacing cover.

Reconnect generator, coil and plug leads.

Clean the carburettor in accordance with the Amal Hints and Tips folder.

Re-assemble the controls to the carburettor before mounting the carburettor onto engine.

Reconnect petrol pipe.

Thread on the chain and secure as previously detailed then fit the shock absorber cover and secure by the two $\frac{1}{4}''$ B.S.F. bolts and split washers.

Fit the exhaust pipes and silencers and if necessary fit new copper washers at the exhaust ports.

Tighten all nuts and bolts securely.

Reconnect battery leads.

A FINAL CHECK OVER OF THE INSTALLATION OF THE POWER UNIT SHOULD BE MADE BEFORE PROCEEDING FURTHER.

Re-starting after Overhaul

Fill the engine sump and gearbox with correct grade of lubricant, remove machine from trestle, flood carburettor and start the machine. Do not ' rev ' the engine but allow it to run at a moderate speed. When on the road a modified running-in procedure should be adopted depending on the nature and amount of parts renewed.

Frame

The front and rear suspension is by spring loaded damper units mounted in rubber bonded bushes as are both the front and rear swinging forks and require no maintenance attention.

Dismantling Wheel Spindles and Bearings

Only in the event of ball bearing wear or other unusual circumstances should the bearing arrangements of the wheel hubs be disturbed. Great care should be taken to ensure that the various washers and distance pieces are correctly re-positioned, that the hub shells are lightly packed with the correct grade of grease, and that the bearing retaining nuts are thoroughly tightened. Reference to the illustrations in the Spares Catalogue will clearly show the general arrangement.

Front Wheel

The bearings are fitted to a hollow spindle and separated by a distance tube, the assembly being retained within the hub by the bearing nut which has its outer face drilled for either a peg spanner or drift. When this nut has been removed, the hollow spindle may be drifted through, allowing the two bearings, distance tube, spacing washer, felt washers and dust cap to be removed. Re-assembly is a reversal of this procedure.

Rear Wheel

The rear wheel spindle has an increased diameter in the centre against which both bearings abut, the bearings being locked in position by a nut at each end. Behind each nut is a spacing washer, an oil seal and a spacer to separate the seal from the bearing. The spindle may be removed by unscrewing either of the nuts, when it may be drifted out leaving one bearing in the hub. It will be noted that there is a distance piece inside the speedometer gearbox and another inside each oil seal. The spacing washer between the left hand bearing nut and brake anchor plate is similar to that used behind the bearing nuts. More than one may be necessary to provide sufficient clearance between the anchor plate and the brake drum.

FAULT FINDING CHARTS

The charts on the following pages provide a logical method of diagnosing any trouble or fault which is likely to arise.

In most cases the rider will be able to remedy the fault as soon as it is discovered, but in case further information is required it will be found on the pages to which reference is made.

Where the remedy is obvious, for example, ' Sparking plug loose ' no further comment is made.

ENGINE STOPS OF OWN ACCORD

		See page
No petrol at carburettor	Petrol tank drained	53
	Petrol tap accidentally closed	53
	Petrol system blocked	53
	Air holes in petrol tank cap, blocked	53
	Air holes in top of carburettor float chamber blocked	53
	Air leak in induction system	48
	Carburettor flooding	53
Petrol at carburettor	Choked main jet	21
	Spark plugs not firing	53
	Contact breaker arm sticking or points require attention	21
	Internal failure in generator, distributor, coil or battery	56

Fig. 11. *Fault Finding*

ENGINE WILL NOT START

See page

- No petrol at carburettor when tickler depressed
  - Tank empty 8
  - Petrol tap not opened .. 9
  - Petrol system blocked .. 53
- Petrol reaching carburettor
  - Spark at plugs
    - Mixture too rich
      - Tickler used unnecessarily .. 9
      - Carburettor flooding .. 53
      - Air filter choked .. 53
    - Mixture too weak
      - Controls not set for starting .. 9
      - Air leaks 47
      - Jets blocked 21
    - Spark too weak to fire under compression
      - Dirty contact breaker points .. 21
      - Leakage in high tension leads .. 54
      - Electrical leakage at spark plugs .. 53
  - Spark at plug terminals
    - Defective, dirty or wet plugs .. 21
  - No spark at plug points
    - Contact breaker arm sticking or points dirty .. 21
    - Short in H.T. leads .. 54
    - Short in switch lead .. 54
    - Failure in insulation .. 54
  - No spark at plug terminals
    - Sparking plug loose .. 16
    - Valve clearance out of adjustment .. 16
    - Valves sticking open .. 22
    - Cylinder head—joint leaking .. 23
  - Poor compression
    - Piston rings gummed in

Fig. 12. *Fault Finding*

ENGINE RUNS INCORRECTLY

		See page
Engine runs steadily but lacks power	Valve clearances require adjustment	16
	Ignition retarded	35
	Valves sticking open	16
	Cylinder head—joint leaking	22
	Piston rings gummed in	23
Engine hunts	Weak mixture	48
	Ignition too far advanced	35
Engine pinks or knocks	Sparking plugs sooted	53
	Ignition too far advanced	35
	Weak mixture	48
	Engine overheating, requiring decarbonising	22
Engine runs erratically — Starved carburettor	Petrol tank cap air vent blocked	53
	Obstruction in petrol system	53
Engine misfires	Faulty spark plugs	53
	Weak mixture	48
	Contact breaker points dirty or incorrect gap	21
	Occasional short in H.T. lead	53
Noises in Engine		55

Fig. 13. *Fault Finding*

Faults and Defects—Causes and Remedies
Petrol System Blocked or Choked

Make sure that the tank is not empty, that the tap is turned on, and that the ventilation hole in the filler cap is not blocked. Disconnect the petrol pipe at the top of the float chamber and if petrol does not flow readily close the tap and dismantle the entire system from tap to carburettor. Clear the pipe with a length of wire. Refit and check. If petrol still does not flow readily, drain off petrol, unscrew petrol tap and dismantle. Clean the tap and its filter. Strain petrol before returning to tank.

Carburettor. Rich Mixture

Should the mixture be too rich for starting, close the petrol tap, open the throttle, make sure the carburettor is not choked, and rotate the engine.

This will clear the cylinders. The engine may start while cleaning out the rich mixture. If it does, open the petrol tap and proceed normally. Otherwise remove the plugs, clean and replace, and start again in the normal manner.

If an air cleaner is fitted, and this appears to be choked, remove filter, wash in petrol, and dip in engine oil, allow surplus to drain away before replacing. For all other carburation faults consult Amal leaflet supplied with the machine.

Ignition System

If the ignition system is thought to be the cause of difficult starting, or faulty running, close the petrol tap and examine the complete system, starting at the sparking plug as follows:

Sparking Plugs

Remove the sparking plugs from the cylinder heads and lay them on the engine so that the points will be visible when the engine is turned. Connect the H.T. leads. Steadily turn the engine and observe the sparking, which should occur regularly at the points. If the spark is irregular or jumps inside the plug body, dismantle, examine and clean the plugs as previously instructed in the section on 'Running Adjustments.' If there is no spark at the plug, disconnect suppressor cap from the plug, unscrew it from the lead and hold the lead so that there is a $\frac{3}{16}"$ gap between the end of the plug lead and any metal part of the engine. Turn the engine and sparks should regularly jump across the gap. If the sparking is irregular or no sparking occurs the trouble must be in the distributor and reference should be made to the contact breaker paragraph. (See Miller Booklet).

H.T. LEADS

A flaw may develop in the insulation of the leads or, after prolonged service, the rubber insulation may perish, allowing the core of the high tension cable to short to earth. A very careful examination of the connections and cable should be made. Examine the contact breaker as previously advised and the high tension pick-up segments and rotor arm. Make sure everything is clean and in correct adjustment.

EXCESSIVE OIL CONSUMPTION

After a considerable period of operation and dependent upon the usage of the machine, the pistons, rings and barrels are likely to be worn, allowing an excessive quantity of oil to pass the pistons and become burnt in the combustion chambers. This will be evident from the blue smoke emitted from the exhaust. When new pistons and rings are fitted or cylinders have been rebored, the oil consumption will still be above normal for a period, but with careful running-in the components will become bedded together and the oil consumption will revert to normal. External losses due to leaks are easily traceable. Be certain, when rebuilding the engine that the the washers at all joints are in good condition. Some of the places most likely to leak and therefore requiring particular attention when re-assembling are:

(*a*) Crankcase joints.

(*b*) Oil pump cover joint.

(*c*) Cylinder base joints.

(*d*) Timing cover joint.

(*e*) Gearbox footchange mechanism cover.

(*f*) The felt washer at chain sprocket end of gearbox final drive shaft.

(*g*) The oil seal at flywheel end of the crankshaft in clutch cam spigot.

(*h*) The breather (in generator cover) which, if faulty will allow crankcase pressure to build up.

NOISES

After a short experience in running the machine the rider will become familiar with the normal sound, and will quickly detect any extraneous noise due to a fault. For example, a noisy engine will result if the valve clearances are not adjusted correctly, or if the adjustment on the rocker tappet screws has not been locked correctly. If a metallic noise is heard, it is probably due to one of the following causes.

(*a*) Engine components not properly secured.

(*b*) Engine components which, through long service, have been worn and slack.

(*c*) Mechanical defect internally.

Any unusual noise should be investigated immediately and it is important that the renewal of components, or other appropriate action, is carried out without delay.

Guarantee

WARRANTY

The Company warrants that in the manufacture of new vehicles and engines all precautions have been taken which are usual and reasonable to secure excellence of materials and workmanship and undertakes that if any defect is disclosed in any part of the same within six months of the date of delivery to the retail customer it will (provided such defective part is returned to the works carriage paid) examine the part alleged to be defective and if on such examination the fault is found to be due to defective materials or workmanship for which it is responsible it will repair or replace the defective part free of charge.

This Warranty is given only in respect of a vehicle or engine purchased by the retail customer as new, for which the Company's current retail List Price has been paid.

The foregoing Warranty is in lieu of any Warranty (or Condition) whether expressed or implied by Common Law, Statute or otherwise as to the description, quality or fitness for their purpose of any goods sold, replaced or repaired by the Company every such Warranty (or Condition) whether expressed or implied being in all cases excluded and the liability of the Company under the terms of this Warranty is strictly limited to the replacement or repair and despatch to the Sender carriage forward of the part replaced or repaired. The Company shall not be responsible for any other liability, expenses, damages, or loss which may occur consequent upon any misdescription, defective material or workmanship of any description.

The Warranty shall be void if the goods are fitted with any part not made by Douglas (Kingswood) Limited. Any vehicle fitted with a body not approved by us is not covered by this or any Warranty.

No Warranty shall apply to defects caused or arising under the following conditions:

- (*a*) During or caused by racing or any other competitive event.
- (*b*) Wear and tear, accident, misuse or neglect or failure to follow the instructions contained in the Instruction Books, if any.
- (*c*) Defects in any vehicle or engine which has been altered in any manner whatsoever or upon which the identification numbers have been altered or removed.
- (*d*) Defects in any vehicle or engine which has been or is let out on hire.
- (*e*) The use of unsuitable fuel or lubricants.
- (*f*) The operation of the vehicle or engine in excess of its rated capacity or under conditions detrimental to its successful operation or likely to cause excessive wear and tear.

This Warranty shall be construed as including and is limited to:

- (*a*) Vehicles or engines bought direct from the Company or from one of its duly authorised Distributors, Dealers or Retail Dealers.
- (*b*) Repairs done or replacements supplied by the Company direct.

The Company gives no Warranty of any description in respect of any Second-hand Vehicles or Engines.

All Agreements and quotations by the Company to supply goods, execute repairs or make replacements shall be deemed to include the above Warranty and to exclude all expressed or implied Warranties and/or Conditions.

The Company does not warrant the Specialities of other manufacturers fitted to its vehicles such as tyres, electrical fittings, lamps and horns. It endeavours to secure satisfactory quality in these articles and the Makers whose names usually appear thereon are generally willing to replace any defective part. The Company will be pleased at all times to furnish the Maker's name and address.

In the Export Market and in lieu of any Warranty or Condition implied by Law we give a Warranty in similar terms (delivering the new parts F.O.B. English Port) to our distributors to whom alone the purchaser must look for his Warranty and for service.

CONDITIONS OF WARRANTY

If a defective part be found in any vehicle or engine it must be sent to the Company, Douglas (Sales & Service) Ltd., Kingswood, Bristol, carriage paid and accompanied by an intimation from the Sender in writing that he desires to have it repaired or replaced free of charge under this Warranty. The Sender must also furnish at the same time:

(a) The number of the vehicle or engine.
(b) The name of the Dealer, if any, from whom he purchased.
(c) The date of the purchase or the date when the repairs were executed or replacements made as the case may be.

The sender shall accept the Company's decision as final and conclusive on all claims for replacement or repairs, under this Warranty.

If these conditions are not strictly complied with, the goods received by the Company will be at the risk of the Sender and this Warranty shall not be enforceable.

The Company shall not be responsible for the cost of any labour involved in connection with the removal or replacement of any defective parts from or to any vehicle or engine. Replaced parts become the Company's property.

Vehicles sent for repairs will only be driven by the Company's employees at the risk and responsibility of the owners and repairs are undertaken only on the assumption that the owners give authority to drive the vehicles on their behalf.

The Company accepts no responsibility for damage by fire or otherwise to customers' vehicles or engines or parts thereof whilst on the Company's premises.

DOUGLAS (SALES AND SERVICE) LTD., KINGSWOOD, BRISTOL
ENGLAND

TELEPHONE 73013/8

ARE YOU:
INTERESTED IN EUROPEAN, IMPORT & EXOTIC AUTOMOBILES?

DO YOU:
DO YOUR OWN MAINTENANCE?

If you answered yes to either of these questions, then you should check out our automobile books and manuals. We have included a sample listing of some of our featured marques. However, for complete details and the most up-to-date information, please visit our website.

—— www.VelocePress.com ——

The fastest growing specialist USA publisher of niche market automotive books and manuals.

All VelocePress titles are available through your local independent bookseller, Amazon.com or direct from VelocePress. Wholesale customers may also purchase direct or from the Ingram Book Group.

AUTOBOOKS WORKSHOP MANUALS

ALFA ROMEO GIULIA 1300, 1600, 1750, 2000 1962-1978 WSM
AUSTIN HEALEY SPRITE, MG MIDGET 1958-1980 WSM
BMW 1600 1966-1973 WSM
BMW 2000 & 2002 1966-1976 WSM
BMW 2500, 2800, 3.0 & 3.3 1968-1977 WSM
BMW 316, 320, 320i 1975-1977 WSM
BMW 518, 520, 520i 1973-1981 WSM
FIAT 1100, 1100D, 1100R & 1200 1957-1969 WSM
FIAT 124 1966-1974 WSM
FIAT 124 SPORT 1966-1975 WSM
FIAT 125 & 125 SPECIAL 1967-1973 WSM
FIAT 126, 126L, 126 DV, 126/650 & 126/650 DV 1972-1982 WSM
FIAT 127 SALOON, SPECIAL & SPORT, 900, 1050 1971-1981 WSM
FIAT 128 1969-1982 WSM
FIAT 1300, 1500 1961-1967 WSM
FIAT 131 MIRAFIORI 1975-1982 WSM
FIAT 132 1972-1982 WSM
FIAT 500 1957-1973 WSM
FIAT 600, 600D & MULTIPLA 1955-1969 WSM
FIAT 850 1964-1972 WSM
JAGUAR E-TYPE 1961-1972 WSM
JAGUAR MK 1, 2 1955-1969 WSM
JAGUAR S TYPE, 420 1963-1968 WSM
JAGUAR XK 120, 140, 150 MK 7, 8, 9 1948-1961 WSM
LAND ROVER 1, 2 1948-1961 WSM
MERCEDES-BENZ 190 1959-1968 WSM
MERCEDES-BENZ 220/8 WSM
MERCEDES-BENZ 220B 1959-1965 WSM
MERCEDES-BENZ 230 1963-1968 WSM
MERCEDES-BENZ 250 1968-1972 WSM
MERCEDES-BENZ 280 1968-1972 WSM
MG MIDGET TA-TF 1936-1955 WSM
MINI 1959-1980 WSM
MORRIS MINOR 1952-1971 WSM
PEUGEOT 404 1960-1975 WSM
PORSCHE 911 1964-1973 WSM
PORSCHE 911 1970-1977 WSM
RENAULT 16 1965-1979 WSM
RENAULT 8, 10, 1100 1962-1971 WSM
ROVER 3500, 3500S 1968-1976 WSM
SUNBEAM RAPIER, ALPINE 1955-1965 WSM
TRIUMPH SPITFIRE, GT6, VITESSE 1962-1968 WSM
TRIUMPH TR2, TR3, TR3A 1952-1962 WSM
TRIUMPH TR4, TR4A 1961-1967 WSM
VOLKSWAGEN BEETLE 1968-1977 WSM

BROOKLANDS BOOKS & ROAD TEST PORTFOLIOS (RTP)

AC CARS 1904-2009
ALFA ROMEO 1920-1933 ROAD TEST PORTFOLIO
ALFA ROMEO 1934-1940 ROAD TEST PORTFOLIO
BRABHAM RALT HONDA THE RON TAURANAC STORY
BUGATTI TYPE 10 TO TYPE 40 ROAD TEST PORTFOLIO
BUGATTI TYPE 10 TO TYPE 251 ROAD TEST PORTFOLIO
BUGATTI TYPE 41 TO TYPE 55 ROAD TEST PORTFOLIO
BUGATTI TYPE 57 TO TYPE 251 ROAD TEST PORTFOLIO
DELAHAYE ROAD TEST PORTFOLIO
FERRARI ROAD CARS 1946-1956 ROAD TEST PORTFOLIO
FIAT 500 1936-1972 ROAD TEST PORTFOLIO
FIAT DINO ROAD TEST PORTFOLIO
HISPANO SUIZA ROAD TEST PORTFOLIO
HONDA ST1100/ST1300 PAN EUROPEAN 1990-2002 RTP
JAGUAR MK1 & MK2 ROAD TEST PORTFOLIO
LOTUS CORTINA ROAD TEST PORTFOLIO
MV AGUSTA F4 750 & 1000 1997-2007 ROAD TEST PORTFOLIO
TATRA CARS ROAD TEST PORTFOLIO

VELOCEPRESS AUTOMOBILE BOOKS & MANUALS

ABARTH BUYERS GUIDE
AUSTIN-HEALEY 6-CYLINDER WSM
BMW 600 LIMOUSINE FACTORY WSM
BMW 600 LIMOUSINE OWNERS HAND BOOK & SERVICE MANUAL
BMW ISETTA FACTORY WSM
BOOK OF THE CARRERA PANAMERICANA - MEXICAN ROAD RACE
DIALED IN - THE JAN OPPERMAN STORY
FERRARI 250/GT SERVICE AND MAINTENANCE
FERRARI 308 SERIES BUYER'S AND OWNER'S GUIDE
FERRARI BERLINETTA LUSSO
FERRARI BROCHURES AND SALES LITERATURE 1946-1967
FERRARI BROCHURES AND SALES LITERATURE 1968-1989
FERRARI GUIDE TO PERFORMANCE
FERRARI OPP, MAINTENANCE & SERVICE H/BOOKS 1948-1963
FERRARI OWNER'S HANDBOOK
FERRARI SERIAL NUMBERS PART I - ODD NUMBERS TO 21399
FERRARI SERIAL NUMBERS PART II - EVEN NUMBERS TO 1050
FERRARI SPYDER CALIFORNIA
FERRARI TUNING TIPS & MAINTENANCE TECHNIQUES
HOW TO BUILD A FIBERGLASS CAR
HOW TO BUILD A RACING CAR
IF HEMINGWAY HAD WRITTEN A RACING NOVEL
JAGUAR E-TYPE 3.8 & 4.2 WSM
LE MANS 24 (THE BOOK THAT THE FILM WAS BASED ON)
MASERATI BROCHURES AND SALES LITERATURE
MASERATI OWNER'S HANDBOOK
METROPOLITAN FACTORY WSM
MGA & MGB OWNERS HANDBOOK & WSM
OBERT'S FIAT GUIDE
PERFORMANCE TUNING THE SUNBEAM TIGER
PORSCHE 356 1948-1965 WSM
PORSCHE 912 WSM
SOUPING THE VOLKSWAGEN
TRIUMPH TR2, TR3, TR4 1953-1965 WSM
VEDA ORR'S NEW REVISED HOT ROD PICTORIAL
VOLKSWAGEN TRANSPORTER, TRUCKS, STATION WAGONS WSM
VOLVO 1944-1968 ALL MODELS WSM

VELOCEPRESS MOTORCYCLE BOOKS & MANUALS

AJS SINGLES 1955-65 350cc & 500cc (BOOK OF)
ARIEL 1939-1960 4 STROKE SINGLES (BOOK OF)
ARIEL LEADER & ARROW 1958-1964 (BOOK OF)
ARIEL MOTORCYCLES 1933-1951 WSM
ARIEL PREWAR MODELS 1932-1939 (BOOK OF)
BMW M/CYCLES R26 R27 (1956-1967) FACTORY WSM
BMW M/CYCLES R50 R50S R60 R69S (1955-1969) FACTORY WSM
BSA BANTAM (BOOK OF)
BSA ALL FOUR-STROKE SINGLES & V-TWINS 1936-1952 (BOOK OF)
BSA OHV & SV SINGLES - 250cc 1954-1970 (BOOK OF)
BSA OHV & SV SINGLES 1945-54 250-600cc (BOOK OF)
BSA OHV SINGLES 350 & 500cc 1955-1967 (BOOK OF)
BSA PRE-WAR MODELS TO 1939 (BOOK OF)
BSA TWINS 1948-1962 (BOOK OF)
BSA TWINS 1962-1969 (SECOND BOOK OF)
DOUGLAS PRE-WAR ALL MODELS 1929-1939 (BOOK OF)
DOUGLAS POST-WAR ALL MODELS 1948-1957 FACTORY WSM
DUCATI 160cc, 250cc & 350cc OHC MODELS FACTORY WSM
HONDA 50 ALL MODELS UP TO 1970 (BOOK OF)
HONDA 90 ALL MODELS UP TO 1966 (BOOK OF)
HONDA MOTORCYCLES 125-150 TWINS C/CS/CB/CA WSM
HONDA MOTORCYCLES 250-305 TWINS C/CS/CB WSM
HONDA MOTORCYCLES C100 SUPER CUB WSM
HONDA MOTORCYCLES C110 SPORT CUB 1962-1969 WSM
HONDA TWINS & SINGLES 50cc to 305cc 1960-1966 (BOOK OF)
LAMBRETTA ALL 125 & 150cc MODELS 1947-1957 (BOOK OF)
LAMBRETTA LI & TV MODELS 1957-1970 (SECOND BOOK OF)
MATCHLESS 350 & 500cc SINGLES 1945-1956 (BOOK OF)
MATCHLESS 350 & 500cc SINGLES 1955-1966 (BOOK OF)
NORTON 1938-1956 (BOOK OF)
NORTON DOMINATOR TWINS 1955-1965 (BOOK OF)
NORTON MOTORCYCLES 1957-1970 FACTORY WSM
NORTON PREWAR MODELS 1932-1939 (BOOK OF)
ROYAL ENFIELD 736cc INTERCEPTOR FACTORY WSM
ROYAL ENFIELD 250cc & 350cc SINGLES 1958-1966 (SECOND BOOK OF)
SUZUKI 50cc & 80cc UP TO 1966 (BOOK OF)
SUZUKI T10 1963-1967 FACTORY WSM
SUZUKI T20 & T200 1965-1969 FACTORY WSM
TRIUMPH PRE-WAR MOTORCYCLE 1935-1939 (BOOK OF)
TRIUMPH MOTORCYCLES 1937-1951 WSM
TRIUMPH MOTORCYCLES 1945-1955 FACTORY WSM
TRIUMPH TWINS 1956-1969 (BOOK OF)
VELOCETTE ALL SINGLES & TWINS 1925-1970 (BOOK OF)
VESPA 1951-1961 (BOOK OF)
VINCENT MOTORCYCLES 1935-1955 WSM

www.VelocePress.com

Please check our website:

www.VelocePress.com

for a complete
up-to-date list of
available titles

www.ingramcontent.com/pod-product-compliance
Lightning Source LLC
Chambersburg PA
CBHW070554170426
43201CB00012B/1841